DESIGN SPIRITS

DESIGN SPIRITS
BARS, BREWPUBS & TECHNO CLUBS

GAIL BELLAMY

Interior Details

AN IMPRINT OF
PBC INTERNATIONAL, INC.

Distributor to the book trade in the United States and Canada
Rizzoli International Publications Inc.
300 Park Avenue South
New York, NY 10010

Distributor to the art trade in the United States and Canada
PBC International, Inc.
One School Street
Glen Cove, NY 11542

Distributor throughout the rest of the world
Hearst Books International
1350 Avenue of the Americas
New York, NY 10019

Library of Congress Cataloging–in–Publication Data

Bellamy, Gail
    Design spirits : bars, brewpubs & techno clubs / by Gail Bellamy
        p.   cm.
    Includes index.
    ISBN 0–86636–375-0 (hb : alk. paper) —— ISBN 0-86636-426-9 (pb :
alk. paper)
    1. Bars (Drinking establishments)—Decoration. 2. Interior
decoration— History—20th century. 3. Interior architecture—
History—20th century. I. Title
NK2195.R4B45 1995   95–13000
725'.7—dc20   CIP

CAVEAT– Information in this text is believed accurate, and will pose no
problem for the student or casual reader. However, the author was often
constrained by information contained in signed release forms, information
that could have been in error or not included at all. Any misinformation
(or lack of information) is the result of failure in these attestations. The
author has done whatever is possible to insure accuracy.

Color separation by Fine Arts Repro House Co., Ltd., Hong Kong
Printing and binding by C&C Joint Printing Co., (H.K.) Ltd., Hong Kong

10 9 8 7 6 5 4 3 2 1

Printed in Hong Kong

To my husband, Stephen Paul Bellamy

CONTENTS

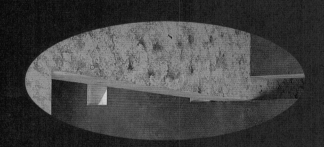

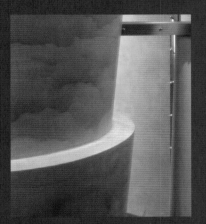

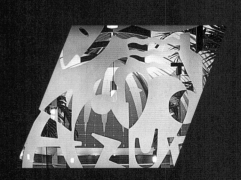

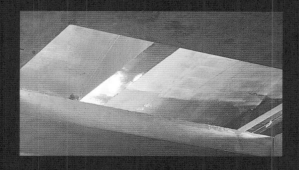

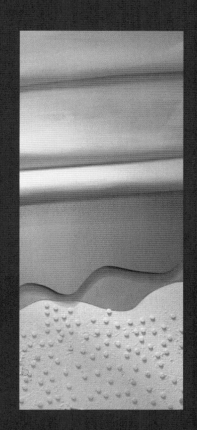

BAR TALK

...**E**xcellence in design develops from a thorough understanding of the project's requirements to develop a functional and aesthetically pleasing space. With a trend towards lower alcohol consumption, specialty bars, such as coffee houses, have become mainstream in our society.

The use of natural materials and inexpensive materials in a new way has become necessary to accommodate clients' restrictive budgets....

Miller Rausch Interior Architecture

...**P**atrons must also be provided with choices; they might want to sit in relative privacy, or they might want to be out in the fray. A well-designed drinking place is a versatile and socially acceptable destination....

Current trends...involve controlling the entire environment through lighting, sound, seating options, technology.

Over the past two decades, bar design has come to emphasize wine and beer and food. Drinking establishments sell more chilled beverages and thus have a need for greater storage capacity. Space needs haven't really changed, but there is a greater demand for variety and comfort. Bars have gotten lighter and more presentable, and more bars are selling food.

Engstrom Design Group

During the past 20 years, eating out has replaced the theater as a source of entertainment, and restaurant/nightspot design is changing as restaurateurs are spending more to create a sense of place. The atmosphere and presence of a restaurant are now as important as the food served. In order to compete, restaurateurs are allowing their designers to be more bold, giving each space a distinctive personality....

Hardy Holzman Pfeiffer Associates

...**D**rinking spaces in the '90s seem to fall into several categories: neighborhood bars; bar/entertainment/amusement centers; nouveau bohemian bar/coffee shop environments, and spaces featuring live music. Each of these project types has a different personality. The "dressed to kill" and "see and be seen" type of disco, pick-up and fern bars of the '70s and '80s are being replaced with lower-key, more casual drinking establishments. People generally aren't drinking as much as they used to, bars are no longer offering huge happy-hour spreads encouraging the after-work crowds, and dancing seems to be decreasing in popularity at nightclubs, with the exception of retro clubs with "Disco Hell" nights.

KRA, Inc.

Current night spots have become more of a gathering place, reminiscent of the local neighborhood bar. People go to relax and intermingle instead of to be in a fashion show. We try to create a space that will complement this philosophy, using warm earth tones and an open roomy atmosphere instead of a closed and sectioned one—a place where people can do many things under one roof: dance, play pool, eat, or just talk with friends.

PeterHansRea

There are, of course, many standards of excellence in planning, in materials, in design, etc. One that consistently stands out is appropriateness—does the combination of planning, materials, design, etc., effectively contribute to the uncovering of the genius of the place? Has the architect read the situation accurately, and has he/she responded meaningfully. That is not to suggest that appropriateness means doing the correct thing. Sometimes a lack of piousness, of appropriateness, is very… appropriate….

Bentel & Bentel, Architects/Planners A.I.A.

The designer must capture and hold the guest's attention, stimulating the visual senses as powerfully as the food does the taste buds. Simply being present in the room should make the occasion an event. A drinking place must provide its patrons with the opportunity to escape the stresses of the day, but it also must offer them comfort and a sense of belonging typically associated with a neighborhood pub or tavern.…

Marve Cooper Design

Bars have become the sole gathering place in this period of time when so many of the traditional meeting places have been lost. The bar is no longer the heavy drinking place. Instead, it's where people go to meet friends, chat, and share companionship.

Today's new drinking laws have had a tremendous impact on bar owners' view of their establishments. Still paramount is the need to draw customers in and get them to spend their money—only now there has to be another draw—heavy drinking is passé. To keep the clientele, bars must have other ways to encourage customers to visit them. Bars have become more entertaining. As an example, sports bars have televisions, memorabilia, and games. The interiors are more welcoming to women—a comfortable setting for suits or sweaters.

Morris Nathanson Design

INTRODUCTION

Most people don't go to bars because they're thirsty—they go to socialize, to see and be seen. That's why design directions are changing for today's drinking places. The less leisure time we have, the more seriously we take it. In a world of borders and barriers and coloring within the lines, successful bars and nightclubs hint at free-form possibilities. Depending on the market segment, bars can be dramatic, or down-home, or whatever the customer's heart desires.

Nowhere is this trend more evident than in dance places, which are an amalgamation of unfolding fantasy and evolving drama. With increased competition from dining operations that offer an evening's entertainment for the dinner dollar, contemporary clubs and dance places rely on providing a combination of fashion and fun. Dance floors are often interspersed with intimate conversation alcoves and areas for activities such as billiards. Whether it's a return to romance or the forward-looking use of illusion and invention, the successful nightspot allows guests to see themselves in a new, exciting light.

Technology can lend the competitive edge. Lighting and sound systems help alter the atmosphere to impart drama, mystery, or maybe even intrigue, on demand. Acoustics and visuals don't carry the load alone, though. Live entertainment venues include casinos and comedy clubs, supper clubs, and cabarets. Providing multiple moods and activities within a single space—shopping, music, dancing, dining, gaming, and memorabilia displays come to mind—helps keep interest high among clientele.

Not everyone wants high energy experiences, of course. Looking back to a time when they were gathering places for the international traveling set, hotel bars are busy reclaiming some of the grandeur of days gone by. Classic cocktails—many of which were developed in the world's great hotel bars—are making a comeback, too. Drawing from various eras of elegance, these spots manage to make guests feel comfortable, without trying to be all things to everybody. Whether the interior is rich with regional references, or lush with a timeless luxury, lounges in upscale hotels compete favorably with local freestanding facilities because they're serious about serving community residents as well as hotel guests. Add people-watching opportunities to the mix, and it's no wonder that the world's hotel bars retain such allure.

Meanwhile, from their street-smart exteriors to their activity-oriented interiors, casual bars know what drawing power is all about, too. Design draws customers in, and a diversity of offerings keeps them coming back. Alfresco dining, eye-catching neon signage, and windows that allow a peak inside are all elements that say "come on in" to passersby. Inside, color and whimsy set patrons at ease. Light-hearted themes or the theatrical aspects of display cooking can add to the ambiance.

Just as having a "mile-long" bar was *de rigueur* in many of the saloons of America's Old West, casual contemporary restaurants pay particular attention to the ambiance of their bars. The appropriateness of casual clothes and the company of congenial customers is enhanced by the availability of affordable, great renditions of everybody's favorite good-time foods. Bar seating also appeals to solo diners.

Casual style is often motivated by the menu, which is why wood-burning pizza ovens and open kitchens find their way into so many designs. Bars in Mediterranean restaurants might feature wine displays, while it's not unusual for the many moods of Mexico to be reflected in a Mexican restaurant's combination of vivid colors, bold flavors, and lively artwork.

Other places can attribute their popularity to a particular combination of qualities. It's as if someone were repeating an incantation for success: history, mystery, mood, and food. Think of your favorite sophisticated bars—they may well be located in restaurants—and try to analyze what you like about them. Don't overlook the tactile or the olfactory aspects, either.

Today's sophisticated bars go beyond being mere holding tanks for customers who show up early for dinner reservations. Sometimes it's a reverence for the past or a recapturing of the grandeur of yesteryear that makes a bar special. Restaurants are places where things happen, places of personal memories, and just as they're more than places to eat, bars are more than places to drink. Consider the long-lived image of Rick's Place in the film *Casablanca*, or Trader Vic's in California, which gained renown as much for Vic Bergeron's invention of the Mai Tai cocktail as for the restaurant's Polynesian food. Going back even further, Fraunces Tavern in New York City is remembered as the place where George Washington bid farewell to his officers in December, 1783.

Restaurants, hotels and nightspots aren't the only places with busy bars, however. When it comes to specialty locations, is it any wonder that in a world where patrons can do their drinking in restaurants and their eating in bars, they can also find nightclubs in stadiums and cafes in malls?

It's no secret that beverage outlets are cropping up in non-traditional sites, including kiosks, retail establishments, atriums, bookstores and airports. A generation ago, who would have thought it would be possible to go pub-crawling inside a mall? Whatever the setting calls for, design creates the magic that makes customers want to stop and stay awhile.

New ideas are brewing, too. Some bars focus on food styles or entertainment themes, but specialty coffee and craft-brewed beer are stars of the show elsewhere. Coffee bars and brewpubs provide a comfortable place for casual get-togethers. Design-by-the-drink trends acknowledge the drawing power of a single beverage, but that's not the whole story.

Coffee-drinking, for instance, is accompanied by conversation, and perhaps a poetry reading or book discussion. Often small and sometimes quirky, coffee cafes hold equal appeal for regular customers and those who drop by for takeout. Traffic flow and retail displays are important considerations in these operations.

Meanwhile, brewpubs are to drinking what display kitchens are to eating: they reinforce the idea of fresh, regional specialties. Brewing equipment is often incorporated into the design. In fact, approximately 300 brewpubs and brewery restaurants are now operating in the U.S. In many of these spots, there's a sense of neighborhood that rekindles the idea of regionality and reinforces the feeling of belonging. Enthusiastic customers tend to linger longer, and return more often.

Tapas bars, sushi bars, and oyster bars are gaining a bigger following, too, with design focus that often follows the menu. For example, tapas are those versatile, quick-cooking Spanish appetizers that can also serve as snacks or a meal. Accordingly, Spanish-influenced spots often have an all-day atmosphere, casual and convivial. Tasting new foods, trying new beverages, and talking to new people are what such places are all about.

Drink in the following design ideas, and while you're doing so, think of mixology as popular culture, lobby bars as luxurious living rooms, and taverns as the new neighborhood landmarks.

Gail Bellamy

Gotham Hall

Manhattan Express

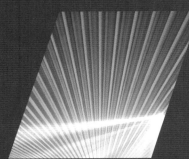

Empire Ballroom

Orchid

"A nightclub operates both as a stage and a haven, giving patrons a venue to show themselves off, and providing a refuge from late 20th century life, which grows more grey and regimented by the day. The goal of good nightclub design is to delight patrons, to enable them to feel that they have never looked better or enjoyed themselves more, and to give them a platform to express themselves freely, as their daily lives almost never permit."

—*Yabu Pushelberg*

Monkey Bar

"... it's the nurturing of our clients' dreams and 'specialness' that gives each project its uniqueness and creates an exciting process. Once we discover the essence of each project, we build on it by integrating the magic and spontaneity of the theatre."

—*Rockwell Architeture, Planning and Design*

Planet Hollywood

OUT ON THE TOWN

HOT SPOTS & TECHNO CLUBS

Gotham Hall

SANTA MONICA, CALIFORNIA

Owner: **Albert & Rene Mizrahi** Designers: **Sam Hatch, Jackie Hanson of Hatch Design Group** Square footage: **9,500** Seats: **225** Opened: **1993** Photographer: **Scott Rothwall**

Gotham Hall is at once majestic and modern, fantasy-like and fashionable, avant-garde and appealing. This billiards nightclub occupies approximately 9,500 square feet on the second level of the refurbished Odd Fellows Building. Enveloping in the same way a magnificent cave might be, rich colors and curvilinearity contribute to the allure. Sweeping lines of accent furnishings and graceful pendant lighting are set against a palette of purple, terra cotta, and green. Metallic accents as well as copper and mesh decorative sconces are found throughout the space. In the restaurant bar area, distinctive dining chairs and exotic lighting fixtures add a decidedly luxurious flair.

Monkey Bar

HOTEL ELYSÉE, NEW YORK, NEW YORK

Architects: **David Rockwell, Alice Yiu, Claire Baldwin of Rockwell Architecture Planning and Design** Square Footage: **3,155** Seats: **50** *(bar)*, **120** *(restaurant)* Opened: **1994** Photographer: **Paul Warchol**

Talk about a concept with staying power, the original Monkey Bar opened in the 1930s. Located in the Hotel Elysée, it drew a celebrity clientele, many of whom resided in the hotel. In the early days, an imposing mahogany bar gave it drama, and panels of mirrors encouraged patrons to mimic themselves, adding a sense of "naughty fun." Later, Charles Vella's caricature murals supplanted the mirrors but the mood was retained.

With the 1994 reopening of the Monkey Bar came the addition of a restaurant. Elements that have been revived include the banana leaf designs stenciled onto a blue linoleum floor, the mahogany bar, the original monkey sconces, and Vella's vibrant murals, now restored. The monkey motif continues in murals and cast bronze railings. A piano in the bar recalls earlier eras in this gathering place, and the fun lives on, too: just look at the barstools that resemble martini olives.

To help imbue the new restaurant with elements of the original concept, a Hirschfeld sketch of well-known customers and waiters at the original Monkey Bar was moved to the dining room. Large New York skyline murals, round Hollywood-style banquettes, deep-toned woods and other details link the restaurant to the bar.

Empire
COSTA MESA, CALIFORNIA
Ballroom

Hard surfaces and softly glowing light work together in a dance club designed to hold as many as 1,000 people at one time. Its designers describe the inspiration as "neoteric post-industrialism." Only the existing perimeter walls and roof were retained in turning a yawning, 13,000-square-foot space into a vibrant club where guests can flow from bars to billiards to dancing. Existing steel window frames in the 40-year-old industrial building were fitted with mirror that replaced the glass. The design team oversaw everything else incorporated into the bare industrial space, too—including seating, bars, and billiard table felt colors. Red and black and light collaborate in the large, activity-oriented space. Traffic flow was carefully routed to avoid bottlenecks.

Owner: **Arpeja** Client: **Jack Litt** Designers:
Rick McCormack, Jackie Hanson of **Hatch
Design Group** Square Footage: **13,000**
Opened: **1994** Photographer: **Cameron
Carothers**

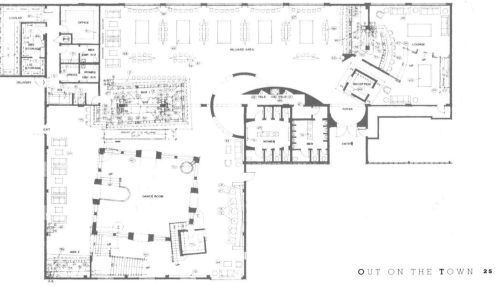

Manhattan Express

First eye-catching, and then enveloping—that's the anatomy of the allure at Manhattan Express. Exciting lighting and a glowing red entry area guide guests who then pass through a black vestibule before arriving in the metallic-walled lobby. Guests wend their way into the nightclub, to the dance floor, to the dining room, or to the smaller caviar bar. The objective was to turn this street-level space of a 5,400-bed Moscow hotel into an international night-club. Interrupted by service shafts, surrounded on three sides by double rows of glass curtain walls, and with less-than-ideal existing electrical and plumbing systems, the physical obstacles of this long, narrow space were many.

Columns, curves, and asymmetry combat the rectangular shape of the space. Bold forms and bright red, blue and purple colors make their overall strong statement. Translucent film covers the glass curtain walls, which now have lights between the rows of glass. In the lounge, intimate lighting levels, a marble bar, the rose glow of the lit drink railing, custom-designed furnishings, and the cheetah-print velvet drapery set a level of sophistication. Laser lighting darts across space and dresses up the raised dance floor. In the café, set off by dramatic blue velvet draperies, guests can slip into the worldly luxury of purple suede booths. A sense of voluptuousness and mystery is created in the more intimate caviar bar. Finally, there's the contrasting sleekness of the VIP room in black and white, with black velvet draperies, black chairs and a zebra-print banquette to set the tone.

Owner: **Kontakt US International** Project
Team: **R. Scott Bromley, Jerry Caldari,
Wing Leung, Nobu Otsu, Christian
Richins, Stephan Russo, John Wender
of Bromley Caldari Architects PC**
Contractor: **FEO Construction and Trade,
Inc.** Consultants *(U.S.)*: **Will Regan/Dave
Rabin, Laszlo Bodak Consulting
Engineers, Full Tilt Productions, Inc.;**
(Russia) **Victor Beletsky, Andre Kostenkov,
SovietInterAchStoy; Masha Sverena;
Gennady Romanov** Square Footage: **10,000**
Design Budget: **$1,000,000** Capacity: **500-
600** Opened: **1993** Photographer:
Elliott Kaufman

Orchid

With both stimulating and soothing elements, this Toronto nightclub combines earthy art and space-age sophistication. The shapes and shades of Orchid, The Nightclub include figurative tableaux influenced by Eastern erotic art. In addition, artists inscribed images on hand-dyed plaster wall surfaces. Graceful curvilinear forms are found from floor to ceiling, and are restated in furnishings as well. Biomorphic shapes seem to flow like the traffic pattern in this intimate yet roomy space that encourages mingling and meandering. While there are numerous conversation niches and observation points, dancing is also appropriate in almost every section of Orchid.

Use of color, scale, and the textures of hand-crafted touches have softened this small-scale industrial space in a building on the edge of Toronto's fashion district. The building itself presented few structural obstacles. Loosely segmented interior spaces—as opposed to structured activity areas—make it a place rich with possibilities. Lighting adds energy to the dance floor with splashes of purple, green, red, and blue. The main bar stretches along a portion of the dance floor perimeter where its cool colors offer an inviting respite for dancers. Another dramatic bar enhances the sophisticated VIP Lounge.

Owners: **Alex Ber, Jim Kambourakis, Dan Pansky, Patrick Rakocovic** Design Firm: **Yabu Pushelberg** Square Footage: **10,800** Capacity: **850** (*nightclub*) Design Budget: **$70,921** Opened: **1995** Photographer: **Robert Burley, Design Archive**

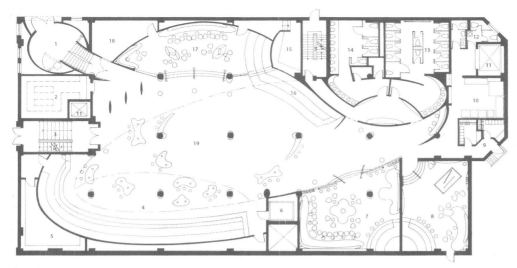

Planet Hollywood, Reno

RENO, NEVADA

If you've ever had sky's-the-limit dreams of ascending into the galactic unknowns of space or descending to the ocean depths in search of sunken treasure, then the imagery of Planet Hollywood, Reno, will speak to your fantasies.

One of 30 Planet Hollywood branches that Rockwell Group was commissioned to design, this facility has successfully integrated the restaurant with a connecting casino. A sunglasses-and-palm-trees sensibility is established as guests enter Planet Hollywood, thanks to the exterior Corinthian columns topped with palm fronds, plus the cheerful pink and green internally illuminated awnings. The design team incorporated a collection of artifacts and employed a variety of lighting techniques in the thematically designed rooms. Back-lighting, optics, accent lighting, and carefully placed fixtures help draw the eye from one beckoning Hollywood-inspired experience to the next.

The casino entry is marked by giant, internally lit pink fiberglass sunglasses. The restaurant's main dining room features a Hollywood Hills "diorama" that combines imagery, nostalgia, lighting effects, and memorabilia. Room themes provide a world of entertainment possibilities, including the Sci-Fi Room, which acknowledges the role of adventure and fantasy in film lore, as well as The Sunken Ship Bar Room and The Sky Room.

Design Team: **David Rockwell, Wade Johnson, Jorge Castillo** of Rockwell Architecture, Planning & Design, P.C. Square Footage: **11,000** Seats: **160** Opened: **1994** Photographer: **Norman McGrath**

Ruby Tuesday

Tuesday

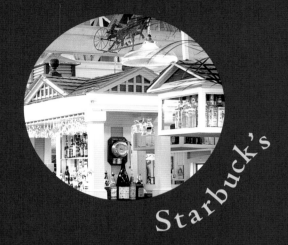

Starbuck's

Winning Streak®

"We believe in creating comfortable environments where people feel welcome and entertained. Bars are no longer dark places populated almost exclusively by men. Patrons have to be stimulated and entertained, whether it's by music, TV, lighting, food, or artwork...."

—Engstrom Design Group

Spinnakers

Bolo

Rio Rio Cantina

"There are places where layers of the past owners and customers have left their mark. We believe the trend is going towards a more simple and refined look that uses long-lasting and rich materials as the foundation. After that, the owners' own quirks become the clothes for the space."

—Sprinkle Robey Architects

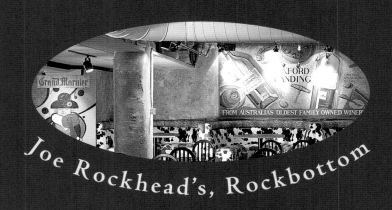

Joe Rockhead's, Rockbottom

Nola's

"A successful drinking place design invites people out of their homes/businesses to share the company of others. It should be comfortable while giving the patron interesting visual objects to enjoy. These visuals should have depth enough that each time the patron visits they might see something new. These visuals should also support the theme of the area, food and drink."

—Miller Rausch Interior Architecture

CHEERS!

CASUAL BARS

Joe Rockhead's, Rockbottom

Eclectic and exuberant, Joe Rockhead's, Rockbottom draws on color, pattern, shapes, textures, and levels—everything up to and including the kitchen sink—in order to appeal to fun lovers of all types. Holstein, Guernsey, jaguar and leopard prints enliven the booth and bar areas. Pool tables and pinball machines add another playful note. Other items used to create the fun atmosphere include a mounted car bumper on one wall, a chalk mural and two permanent beverage-oriented murals. Two stand-up counters contribute to the casual mood. Design here draws away from what was once a dark, divided space suffering from low ceilings and a below-grade location devoid of sidewalk appeal. Three previous operations in this space were unsuccessful. Adding an open kitchen removed the problem of kitchen walls that separated desirable and undesirable sections. Uncovering the windows, providing lighted signage, and adding a three-tiered patio to street level all served to enhance the street presence of the space.

Designer: **Robert Lozowy, Martin Hirschberg Design Associates Ltd.**
Square Footage: **4,800** Design Budget: **$350,000** Photographer: **Interior Images by Richard Johnson**

Ruby Tuesday

BILOXI, MISSISSIPPI

Owner: **Morrison Restaurants, Inc.**
Designer: **Kyle Kieper, FRCH Design
Worldwide (formerly SDI/HTI)** Architect:
**Michael Gabriel, Morrison Restaurants,
Inc.** Square Footage: **1,500** Seats: **75**
Opened: **1994** Photographer:
George Cott/Chroma, Inc.

Victorian details, a timeless view, and visually stimulating design elements join forces to give Ruby Tuesday its up-to-the-moment sense of drama. Deep green and dark wood tones create a rich impression that invites lingering. Leather banquettes, Tiffany lamps, and ceramic tile flooring all summon yesteryear. Seating at the bar, booths, or tall tables creates a variety of experiences for customers. Since many restaurants in the Ruby Tuesday chain have shopping mall locations which don't require windows, this freestanding beachfront prototype required rethinking to take advantage of the Gulf of Mexico view. An outdoor dining deck with seating for 60 capitalizes on the waterfront view.

Starbuck's

Nothing says "come and sit for a spell" the way a front porch does. That's why front porch sociability was built into the plan for this focal-point bar which is slightly elevated from the dining area. It evokes a feeling of belonging that's imparted by places comfortably aged by sun and time. The 1940s Coney Island beach house theme is conveyed by the weathered effect of white-stained wood. Folk art and whimsical touches throughout the interior showcase the owner's artifacts collected from spots along the Cape Cod Highway. Examples include the Fokker airplane in the rafters, and the weather vane atop a miniature back bar house that holds bottles and glassware. All in all, the effect is one of heirlooms in the attic, with intriguing pieces eveywhere.

The design task was to blend two buildings, adding 3,000 square feet to an existing structure that was formerly a nightclub. In the process of marrying a modern addition to an unassuming Cape Cod structure, the intention was to provide a gathering place with staying power, one that would encourage year-round business in this tourist area.

Owner: **Bloom Management Corp.**
Design Firm: **Morris Nathanson Design**
Architect: **Walter Yarosch, Yarosch Associates** Square Footage: **6,300**
Design Budget: **$800,000** Seats: **45** (bar), **240** (total) Opened: **1985** Photographer: **Warren Jagger Photography**

Winning Streak®
Sports Grill

High energy—in the ballpark, on the basketball court, or at the bar—is conducive to entertainment. This sports bar and restaurant concept, part of Harrah's Casino Complex, plays by the international "rules" of having a good time, and its energy level is equally appealing to men and women. Guests are given exciting visuals, a variety of activity choices, and seating options that range from privacy to center stage to observation perches. In addition, each seating area provides a good view of sports programming on television.

Winning Streak®, with its grandstands, field lights, and old stadium ballpark design, promotes sports. The design inspiration comes from Ebbets Field in Brooklyn, circa 1914, with its arched, multiple-paned windows, brickwork, and steel bleacher supports. To overcome budget limitations, low-priced materials were employed to create a rich environment. Inside the complex, railings are modeled after the galvanized barriers at Detroit's Briggs Stadium. Lighting effects create shifting points of view as the ceiling "sky" changes from day to night. Two-

Owner: **The Promus Companies, Harrah's Riverboat Entertainment Division** Design Team: **Eric Engstrom, Jennifer Johanson, Katy Hallal of Engstrom Design Group** Base Building Architecture/Design: **Barry Marshall, Valli Wiggins of Hnedak Bobo Group** Contractor: **John Fox, Larry Thomas of Hensel Phelps** Lighting Design: **Elwyn Gee Group** Square Footage: **2,850** Design Budget: **$366,109** Seats: **141** Opened: **1994** Photographer: **Hank Young**

dimensional sports fans sit in second-story grandstands, and football field colors and markings are captured in the main dining area carpeting. There's a basketball court dining section complete with a hoop, and a centralized shuffleboard court does double duty as a dance floor during the evening.

Video games and a retail area round out the activities. Designers coordinated the purchasing of sports memorabilia, such as Joe Montana's signed Chiefs football and helmet, and old Kansas City Monarchs uniforms. A spatial void at the "stadium" center was filled by the scoreboard focal point which consists of a programmable neon sculpture and eight television monitors. An exhibition kitchen pays tribute to the serious emphasis placed on food.

Spinnakers

True to the sailing reference in its name, antipasto/oyster bar offerings reinforce the Mediterranean seafood menu theme at Spinnakers. Formerly, patrons opted for patio seating instead of the dining room in summer. The idea was to create an indoor impression of outdoor dining and thus encourage year-round business. With the $100,000 retrofit/redesign budget and whirlwind three weeks' construction time for the retrofit, some dramatic design departures were in order.

The resulting interior plays with nontraditional use of color, texture, and materials to create desirable seating areas. Floor slate forms the bar top, and feature-walls boast artistic faux finishes. Metal railings suggest fish nets. In a further break with tradition, ricochets of color carve out unexpected areas of visual interest in the dining room.

Design Team: **Connie Young, Martin Hirschberg** Interior Design: **Martin Hirschberg Design Associates Ltd.** Design Budget: **$100,000** (interior retrofit/redesign) Faux-Finish Artist: **Atelier Danzig** Photographer: **Interior Images by Richard Johnson**

WASHROOM

WASHROOM

Service
Station

Service
Station

To Patio

Back Counter

Refrigerated
Display

Display Shelf

UP

Wait
Station

Service
Bar

Espresso
Cappucino
Maker

Glass
Washer

Bottle
Display

BAR

⑩

⑧

⑦

②

④

⑥

③

Drink
Ledge

⑨

⑪

Oyster
Display

Oyster
Cooker

Display
Shelf

Sliding
Glass
Doors

⑤

①

UP

Sliding
Glass
Doors

Hostess
Station

Bolo

NEW YORK, NEW YORK

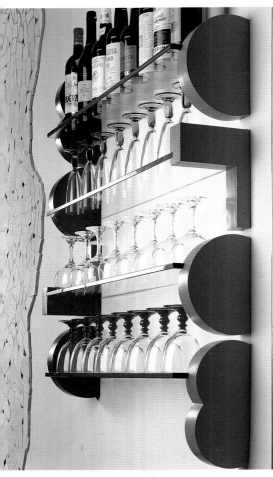

Bolo, named for chef Bobby ("Bo") Flay and developer Laurence ("Lo") Kretchmer, bursts forth with colors and forms that blend New York with Spain. The energetic, expressive interior was inspired by the lively works of Spanish painter Miró, cubist and collage-creator Braque who incorporated pieces of newspaper and fabric into his art, and the Spanish architect Gaudi who favored vivid colors. The Spanish theme is articulated through cuisine as well as color; accordingly, a brick oven is set off by brightly colored tile. Fringe lamps, a mahogany bar, and the bold blue, gold and red color scheme are in keeping with the look. The bar area reinforces the restaurant's theme with details such as the playful glass and bottle rack, and the fact that selected menu items are listed on the back bar mirror. The freeform, silk-screened wallpaper mural is by Alexander Isley; custom wall sconces were designed by the architect.

Owner: **FKBK Restaurant, Inc.** Architects: **James Biber, Michael Zweck-Bronner of Pentagram Design** Graphic Designer: **Alexander Isley, Alexander Isley Design** Square Footage: **2,000** Design Budget: **$250,000** Seats: **82** Opened: **1993** Photographer: **Reven T. C. Wurman**

Rio Rio
SAN ANTONIO, TEXAS
Cantina

Owner: **Joe Cosniac** Design Team: **Davis Sprinkle, Thom Robey, Dwayne Bohuslav, Stephen Smisek, Robert Moritz, Catharine Tarver of Sprinkle Robey Architects** Square Footage: **5,000** Design Budget: **$300,000** Seats: **115** Opened: **1993** Photographer: **Paul Bardagjy**

In keeping with the casual Southwestern connotations of the word cantina, there's nothing shy or stuffy about this nightclub addition to a tourist-area restaurant on San Antonio's Paseo Del Rio. It was the owner's wish that the addition also serve as a banquet area and a daytime restaurant. At first glance, the colors create a tangy, citrusy impression, but at second look, more levels and layers reveal themselves. From the mezzanine dining section to the main staircase and covered outdoor dining area, many people-watching possibilities prevail. A 73-foot-long granite-topped bar meanders like a river throughout the interior, and is reportedly one of the longest bars in Texas.

Although the 120-foot-long, 23-foot-wide space has few windows, there's a carousel quality to the 8-foot-tall custom-wrought iron chandelier, which serves as a shining example of how focal points and vivid colors can create a celebratory atmosphere. Besides the chandelier, custom-wrought iron pieces include wall sconces, the exterior arch, niche lights, and handrails. Tabletops tie in with the red oak ceiling finish; other color touches include the cherry red stained bar stools, and upbeat artwork.

Nola's Cocina Mexicana

PHOENIX, ARIZONA

Modern Mexico serves as the prevailing design metaphor at Nola's. The interior focal point is definitely the bar, glittering with glassware and defined by four flared natural stone columns that mark the bar boundaries. The columns are a unifying element, echoing the entry arches. For all-around conviviality, the idea of an island bar makes sense, surrounded as it is by dining tables. The 14-foot-high ceiling stops in curves just short of the bar, where there's a cavernous 25-foot-high space from which ducts, speakers, and lighting emerge.

Mainly Mexican and modern, yes, but there are also touches that speak of ageless art—the rusted metal bar arches and the use of natural stone. Appetizing tones such as mustard and sage attest to the spirit and flavor of Mexico, while reinforcing the idea of relying on cuisine rather than cliché to create a mood.

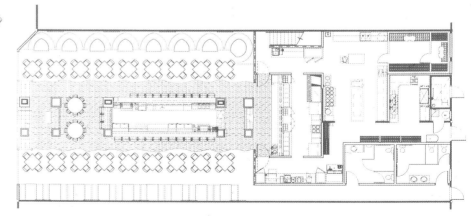

Owners: **Gary Schulz, Roseanne Schulz**
Architects: **Jeffrey Rausch, Kim Dudley**
of Miller Rausch Interior Architecture
Square Footage: **4,709** Design Budget:
$250,000 Seats: **160** Opened: **1994**
Photographer: **Michael Norton**
Photography, Inc.

JUdson Grill

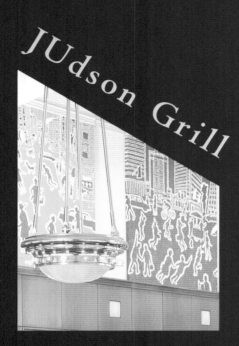

La Placita

Tang's

"We measure
our excellence by
the success of our
clients. If our design
does not lead to a prospering
business, we judge it a failure. . . .
Currently the trend in nightspots
is toward themed entertainment.
In the past such facilities were
built around social interaction;
this is rarely the case now."

—*Shea Architects, Inc.*

Spago

Bossa
Nova

Corner
stone Grill

"Through innovation, style
and function, Cornerstone
Grill transcends common-
place design and enters a
realm all its own."
—*Hatch Design Group*

Luna Notte

TOP-SHELF

SOPHISTICATED BARS

Cornerstone
BREA, CALIFORNIA
Grill

Don't bother pinching yourself; you're not dreaming. The Cornerstone Grill really does have its light-and-shadow fantasy aspects. "Playfully eerie" is how the designers describe it. Architecture reminiscent of New Orleans meets appointments that one might expect to find in a dream castle. The harlequin upholstery fabric on booth backs is just one small example. Brick arches, sconces, and metalwork are counterbalanced by luxurious-looking blue velvet draperies and custom-fabricated furnishings and flooring. Low-voltage lighting combines custom-blown glass and hand-wrought metal housings with dimmers that allow alterations in lighting levels. This space also exceeds ADA requirements, since accessibility was a prime consideration.

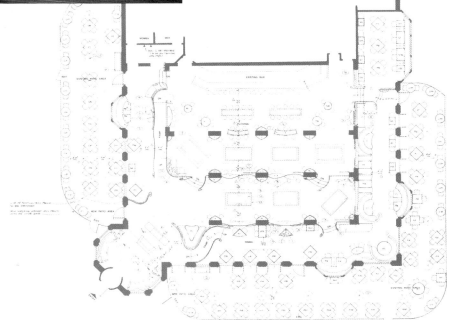

Owner: **Craig Hoffman** Designers: **Sam Hatch, Jackie Hanson of Hatch Design Group** Square Footage: **10,000** Seats: **325** Opened: **1994** Photographer: **Cameron Carothers**

JUdson Grill

Ease balanced with elegance, Manhattan-style, is the message that comes through at JUdson Grill in the Equitable Building on West 52nd Street. The name with its two initial capital letters is derived from the former telephone exchange of this neighborhood known for nightlife. In updating the existing space, Pentagram incorporated existing elements, such as the lighting, with new defining details. A restrained use of color accentuates the grandeur and glamour of the space. High vaulted ceilings, mezzanine dining, and a rounded bar at one end of the main dining floor make for a dramatic interior. Mohair velvet upholstery, dark mahogany, and tall ceramic urns custom designed by the architect work together to maintain the mood. Color accents come from the 6-foot-square murals by artist John Parks.

Owners: **Jerome Kretchmer, Jeff Bliss, Edward G. Brown, Jane Epstein, Christopher Cannon** Architects: **James Biber, Michael Zweck-Bronner of Pentagram Design** Graphic Designer: **Alexander Isley, Alexander Isley Design** Square Footage: **7,500** Design Budget: **$300,000** Seats: **233** Opened: **1994** Photographer: **Reven T. C. Wurman**

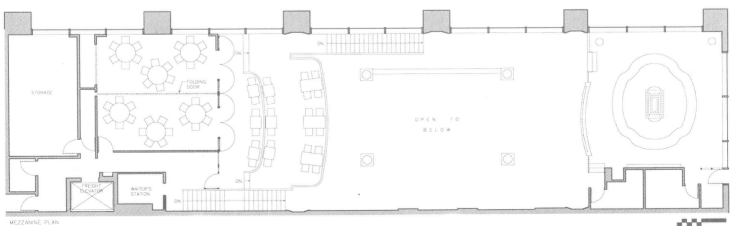

STORAGE

FOLDING
DOOR

FREIGHT
ELEVATOR

WAITER'S
STATION

DN.

DN.

DN.

DN.

OPEN TO
BELOW

MEZZANINE PLAN

0 5 10

La Placita

Mexico meets Hong Kong, in the form of La Placita. The character and color of modern Mexico are evident from the moment one encounters the bright symbols on the entry door. The shapes and styles used throughout the interior offer subtle shades of Mexico. Authentic touches are further expressed in the mix of materials, including terra-cotta flooring and hand-painted wall tiles. Wood ceiling beams do double duty, hiding utilities and providing a sense of openness. Vivid colors and custom lighting fixtures designed by the architect compensate for the lack of natural light in the space. Archways, the water fountain, and tile designs (including those on the bar front) all collaborate to create a Mexican village ambiance in the sunniest sense of the word.

Owner: **Heinz Grabner** Architect: **Steven Lombardi** Square Footage: **7,600** Design Budget: **$200/sq. ft** Seats: **180** Opened: **1994** Photographer: **Kerun Ip**

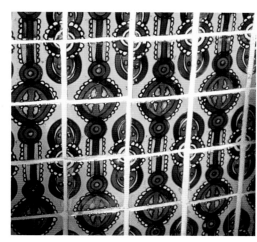

Luna
Notte

One glance tells guests this is a serious wine bar. Wine bins on display at the restaurant's entrance are the launching point for wine references, and a view of the bar catapults customer wine awareness to the next level of interest. Luna Notte's personality balances the use of industrial materials with a blend of human activity, from bar and restaurant patrons to workers in the open kitchen. The slate-floored entranceway leads either to a carpeted dining room or the concrete-floored bar. Industrial materials include galvanized metal and slate-tiled walls, aluminum lighting fixtures, and a curving bar top formed by a single slab of concrete. These aspects peacefully coexist with an open kitchen and free-standing pizza oven that afford guests the opportunity to watch their meals being prepared. Low metal screen partitions extended between concrete counters serve to set the bar area apart from the dining room.

Owner: **Reed Clemons** Architects: **Dick Clark, Chris Lewis of Dick Clark Architecture** Contractor: **APA Construction** Consultant: **Jerry Fleming** Square Footage: **6,500** Seats: **200** Opened: **1991** Photographer: **Paul Bardagjy**

Bossa Nova
CHICAGO, ILLINOIS

There's a delightful, dancing feeling to this world beat supper club where transcultural live music—from samba to salsa to reggae—emanates nightly from an elevated bandstand. And just as jazz interpolations find their way into the Afro-Brazilian bossa nova beat, so do a confluence of design details and international menu influences come together at Bossa Nova.

Mahogany shutters, heavy velvet draping, and warm earth tones leave the impression of sultriness so often associated with Brazil. Both the curving bar and leather banquettes that weave their way along seem to undulate with the dance beat. Gilded mirrors and pinspot lighting with colored gels perpetuate the warm glow of the multi-level space. The tapas menu offers a sampling of island cuisines, plus Spanish, Mediterranean, and Pan-Asian specialties.

Owner: **Restaurant Development Group**
Designer: **Mark Knauer, Knauer Inc.** Seats:
180 *(dining)* Opened: **1992** Photographer:
Jim Yochum

Spago
Las Vegas

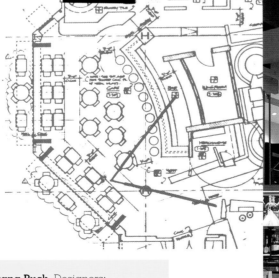

Personality-plus is an appropriate way to describe the panache of the café and bar at Spago Las Vegas. Imagine the expectations: a celebrity chef (Wolfgang Puck); a celebrated sister restaurant of the same name in West Hollywood, California; and the sophisticated surroundings of The Forum Shops at Caesars.

Ornamental metals and mosaic motifs enrich the interior. Spaces in this multilevel Spago include the main dining room with its open kitchen, a 50-seat informal café and bar, and a second-floor balcony, lounge, and private dining area.

In the café and bar, whitewashed wood ceiling beams pay tribute to the interior of the original Spago. At one end, the café bar opens onto The Forum Shops. The primavera wood-topped bar is in front of a glass-enclosed wine room which separates the cafe from the dining room. A copper hood atop the wood-burning pizza oven complements the copper-clad columns elsewhere in the interior. Flooring is scored concrete with inset metal. Marble-topped cafe tables and brightly upholstered chairs contribute to the casual warmth.

Owner: **Wolfgang Puck** Designers:
Adam D. Tihany, Glenn Ondo of Adam D. Tihany International, Ltd. Architect:
Marnell Corrao Associates Contractor:
Pacific Southwest Development Square
Footage: **16,500** Design Budget: **$250/sq. ft.**
Seats: **50** *(café/bar)* Photographer:
Peter Paige

Tang's Ginger Cafe
MINNEAPOLIS, MINNESOTA

Nothing blatant, nothing that shouts, just creativity born of a limited budget and the desire for subtlety of style. That's the story at Tang's, where design provides a progressive American-Oriental cafe environment.

Furnishings and lighting fixtures allude to pagodas and woks, respectively, while the graphics bear elements of Oriental script.

Simplicity and alternative thinking are evident in the details, from floor to ceiling. Start with the dyed concrete floor and move to the particulars of lighting—wall sconces, hung behind mirrored screens, use common lightblubs, and fluorescent tubes are hung sculpturally. Also, hollow metal stock was used for the entry "light poles."
Even the small touches demonstrate a devotion to streamlined simplicity; sleeved bolts function as coat hooks, for instance.

A tilted graphic soffit helps unify the space, while a representational ginger plant/light sculpture establishes a focal point for the dining room.

Owner: **Peggy Tang** Design Team: **Jeffrey P. Agnes, Lynn Forbra, Ryan Haro of Shea Architects** Opened: **1992** Photographer: **Christian Korab**

Diamond Jim's
Premium Palace

Knitting Factory

Iridium

Carolines
Comedy
Club

The Big Life

"Drinking places, like dining places, are part of an evening's (or day's) entertainment. They should be theatrical at some level, even if they simply present the customer with that 'good old neighborhood bar' ambiance. The trend has shifted from 'flashy' to casual and relaxed."

—*Schweitzer BIM*

Country
Star

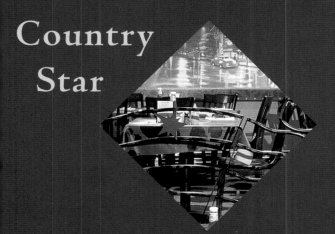

Club Clearview
Art Bar & Cafe

"…Techniques of stage and lighting design are being employed to create a sense of drama. Unusual materials are being used to differentiate spaces. Thematic ideas are being explored to give meaning to the experience of dining out."

—Hardy Holzman Pfeiffer Associates

Rainbow & Stars
Rainbow Room
Rainbow Promenade Bar

Ivory

THAT'S ENTERTAINMENT!

ABARETS, COMEDY CLUBS & OTHER FUN SPOTS

FUKUOKA DOME, FUKUOKA, JAPAN

In The Big Life, a sports bar nightclub at Fukuoka Dome, the fun fans out into 17 themed areas, with a 600-foot-long rail for drinking and eating that overlooks the stadium playing field. In fact, it's said to be the longest sports bar in Japan, although much of the space is only 24 feet wide. Beginning with the murals at the escalator entry, guests can step into a variety of scenes, all of which play off the sports theme. Abstract forms abound, from the blue interior at Seventh Wave, to the ceiling mural at Ringside Bar. There's the Illegal Motion Discotheque, as well as drinking places, food, games, and entertainment, all co-existing in this animated atmosphere where a number of sports have defined the design direction.

Owner: **Daiei** Architect: **Josh Schweitzer,
Schweitzer BIM** Producer: **Sy Chen, CIA**
Square Footage: **20,000** Seats: **1,000**
Opened: **1993** Photographer: **Motoi Niki,
Nacasa & Partners**

Country Star

Beginning with the bigger-than-life experience of entering through the jumbo jukebox exterior, the multiple settings at Country Star give guests the feeling that they're walking around inside the music scene. This is a family fun spot dedicated to country music, with a western design flair. Record album designs are inset into table-tops, and a dining area railing resembles a wavy music staff. Built-in activities include dancing, live entertainment, videos, music, shopping, dining, and taking in the memorabilia displays.

One wall boasts a Nashville street scene mural. Another section, rich with rounded forms, polished wood, and shiny chrome, resembles a giant pinball machine. One of the dining areas is in the style of a stream-lined, traditional diner. Among the variety of scenes created is a rotunda dome, resembling the nighttime desert sky, with added rock formations that give character to the walls. A Grand Canyon palette enriches memorabilia display areas. Star shapes imbedded in the walk-of-fame floor are repeated in bar stool upholstery, and elsewhere in the space.

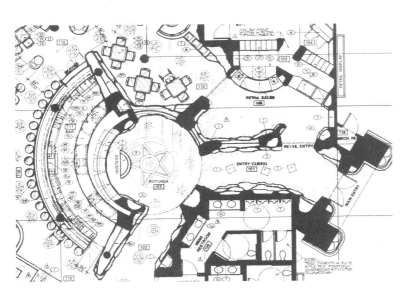

Owner: **Country Star Restaurants, Inc.**
Designers: **Jeff Hatch, Bill Cole, Jackie Hanson Kimberly Gee, Ben Pollock of Hatch Design Group** Square Footage: **15,000** Seats: **530** Opened: **1994**
Photographer: **Cameron Carothers**

Diamond Jim's

TROPWORLD CASINO & ENTERTAINMENT RESORT,

Premium Place

ATLANTIC CITY, N.J.

Starting at the entrance area, reverberations from reflective surfaces, such as black granite flooring and mirrored ceilings, enhance the effect of water walls and create the anticipation of infinite possibilities. Soothing sounds and sensuous surroundings continue throughout the space at Diamond Jim's. Imparting crystal palace elegance, the cascades of water are actually part of a design plan that focused on cost reduction and conveying a sense of novelty and excitement. Floor-to-ceiling walls and columns of water give off a kinetic energy with recirculating water bubbling within and lit from above. These water walls make the most of available space and incorporate the use of colored lights that can change the look. Twenty-two water wall panels—each 2 feet wide and 9 feet high—are combined with an equal number of water columns, each 8 inches in diameter and 9 feet high (measurements include bases), all of which do double duty by serving to create five separate spaces with a sense of motion and liveliness. Furnishings are resplendent with residential sensibilities. The 3,550-square-foot lounge is located on the concourse level. Other dramatic details at TropWorld Casino & Entertainment Resort include the grandeur of torchieres in the casino's 14,000-square-foot concourse, and dramatic 13-foot-tall columns in the 90,800-square-foot casino.

Owner: **TropWorld Casino & Entertainment Resort** Design Firm: **Norwood Oliver Design Associates, Inc.** Square Footage: **3,550** Seats: **87** Opened: **1993** Photographer: **Peter Paige**

Carolines Comedy Club

Given the fact that there's a renaissance of live comedy, it's not surprising to find a richness of Renaissance references to harlequins, court jesters, and jokers throughout Carolines. In fact, to paraphrase the words of the clown in Shakespeare's *Twelfth Night*, humor shines everywhere in this live comedy venue. Images and symbols of the "purveyors of humor" abound.

Neo-medievalism is evident in color and pattern, but the tribute to the history of humor doesn't stop there. From the club's Times Square Broadway entrance, guests descend a grand staircase to the bar video lounge, gaining their first glimpses of the theme along the way. The bar fly stools make light of the bar environment, and names of comedians are etched into a glass soffit above the bar. Traffic flow in this area, with its several intimate sections for drinking and conversation, accommodates crowds who gather for the two nightly performances. Materials such as tapestries, terrazzo, and velvet reinforce the medieval references.

In the tiered comedy theater, there's a decidedly residential ambiance. Contributing to the living room environment are couch-like banquettes and velvet drapes, both of which work together to delineate seating levels. If necessary, the drapes can also serve to subdivide theater areas and close off unused seating sections. The club is designed for both live and televised comedy production.

Owner: **Caroline Hirsch** Design Team: **Paul Haigh, AIA; Barbara Haigh; Nicolas Macri; Miriana Doneva; Karla R. Kupiec; Justin R. Bologna of Haigh Architects Designers** Square Footage: **11,000** Seats: **300** *(club)*, **80** *(restaurant)* Design Budget: **$1.8 million** Opened: **1993** Photographer: **Elliott Kaufman**

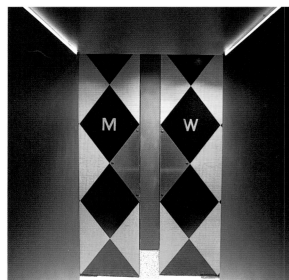

Club Clearview,
Art Bar & Cafe

DALLAS, TEXAS

Like siblings with distinctly different personalities, these nightspots operate under the umbrella of Concept Nouveau.

Club Clearview, designed for low maintenance and versatility, has been open since 1985. The roomy warehouse space is broken up into distinct sections, and interior artwork in the form of paintings, murals, and found objects add personality. The three environments include a live music room, the Blacklight Room with a DJ booth, dance floor, and bar, plus the Video Bar which incorporates a merchandising area.

Think of Art Bar and Cafe as the arty one, a gallery space that's always trying on new looks. Its white walls are a blank palette for art shows, and the mural wrapping around the front of a glass-topped bar can be easily changed.

Owners: **Jeff Swaney, Jeffrey Yarbrough**
Designers: **Jeff Swaney, Jeffrey Yarbrough**
of Concept Noveau Architect: **Bobby**
Garman Opened: **1985** Photographer:
Brian Barnaud

Owners: **Jeff Swaney, Jeffrey Yarbrough**
Designers: **Jeff Swaney, Jeffrey Yarbrough
of Cool Mission III** Architect: **Stephen
Ockels** Opened: **1995** Photographer:
Brian Barnaud

Iridium

If life were a fairy tale, then Iridium would be the dancing dream within it. Music, with its swoops and swirls and arabesques, provides the design vocabulary at this jazz club and restaurant across from Lincoln Center. Ballets, operas, symphonies, jazz groups, and even the components of musical instruments themselves are called upon. Door handles resemble music notes. Handrails owe their appearance to clarinet hardware. Tile flooring designs depict the structure of harmony. Cast aluminum frames of the custom-designed bar stools and chairs suggest they're wearing leg warmers and toe shoes, and ballet-inspired table lamps of bronze and blown glass appear to be wearing tutus.

The fun and fluidity of pop culture are built into the design at Iridium. Shapely bell-bottomed chairs with platform shoes almost resemble upholstered jigsaw puzzle pieces. The five flavors of Chuckles® candy provided color inspirations for furniture upholstery. In addition, the sense of undulating walls and waving arches provide patrons of the television generation with an atmosphere that seems shaped by lens perspective. It's a world where wide-angle distortion and telephoto effect create the illusion of elongated or foreshortened objects. There's a dancing feeling to the bar area as well.

Owner: **Sturm Family** Architects: **Jordan Mozer & Associates, Ltd.** Designer: **Jordan Mozer** Square Footage: **9,000** Design Budget: **$2 million (approximately)** Opened: **1993** Photographer: **Andrew Garn**

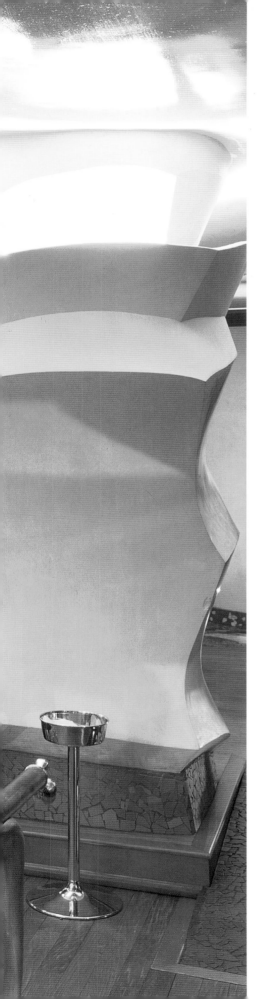

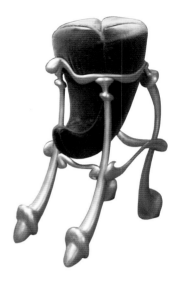

Rainbow & Stars,
NEW YORK, NEW YORK.
Rainbow Room,
Rainbow Promenade Bar

Why rewrite history or reconfigure a rainbow? When the legendary Rainbow Room underwent restoration, the moods, motifs and period details of the 1930s were abstracted and resynthesized to maintain authenticity while preparing this classic nightspot's move into the next millenium. Details such as the milled aluminum, polished bronze, geometric motifs, mahogany woodwork, fabric patterns, leather tints, and artistic use of glass helped retain the splendor of the original style.

The Rainbow Room, Rainbow & Stars, The Rainbow Promenade, and the Rainbow Suites comprise the complex on the 64th and 65th floors of Rockefeller Center called Rainbow. Much detailed research went into the $20 million modernizing project.

The 240-seat Rainbow Room, a formal supper club that first opened in 1934,

remains internationally known. The original crystal chandelier still presides over the revolving dance floor, and windows from floor to ceiling admit extra glitter to the room with a skyline view that extends for 50 miles in every direction.

In the 100-seat Rainbow & Stars, stars of the human type—Tony Bennett and Rosemary Clooney included—perform in the intimate cabaret supper club setting. The starry reflection of Milton Glaser's fiber optic rainbow adds even more sparkle and special magic to the room.

Whether guests choose a cozy table for two or slip onto a seat at the curving mahogany cocktail bar, the golden age of the cocktail lives on at the 120-seat Rainbow Promenade Bar. Hanging from the ceiling is a red and black model of an ocean liner designed by Norman Bel Geddes.

Architect: **Hugh Hardy, FAIA, of Hardy Holzman Pfeiffer Associates** Opened: **1934** (original), **1987** (reopening) Seats: **240** (Rainbow Room), **100** (Rainbow & Stars), **120** (Rainbow Promenade Bar)

Ivory

Think of winks, slinky dresses, late suppers and saxophone solos. Ivory hints at such things, and expresses itself with elements of hedonism and candid excess. Zebra and leopard print rugs, for instance, recall earlier eras of glamour. A sensual supper club ambiance owes part of its flirtatiousness to the diffused light that passes through beaded curtains, fretwork screens, and an organza drapery. The mood moves in, like mist filtering through foliage. All of these details help create cozy conversation areas and intimate dining settings. Sensuous fabrics—striped satin dining chair upholstery and the rich brocades of the banquette seating areas—add a luxurious, tactile dimension.

Owner: **Charles Khabouth** Designers: **George Yabu, Kevin McCall of Yabu Pushelberg** Square Footage: **1,200** Seats: **60** (*bar*), **40** (*dining*) Design Budget: **$350,000** Opened: **1995** Photographer: **Robert Burley, Design Archive**

Knitting Factory

Technology, acoustics, live performances, antiques and artwork join forces to provide a density of experience for guests at the Knitting Factory. The club grew from its original 1980s site in Greenwich Village, and graduated to the current SoHo Landmark District. From its inception, the Knitting Factory has offered a live venue for young, unknown musical artists. The acoustics support live recordings: the walls, ceilings, and floors incorporate sound-proofing and vibration isolation elements. Record covers from in-house performing artists are featured in the center of each custom-built table. Show information is available on the Internet.

Amenities of the four-level facility include a recording studio, a revolving display of original artwork, the Main Room

Architect: **Orli Eshkar, Orli Eshkar Architects** Square Footage: **15,000** Seats: **200/40** Design Budget: **$50,000** Opened: **1994** Photographer: **Gerdi Eller**

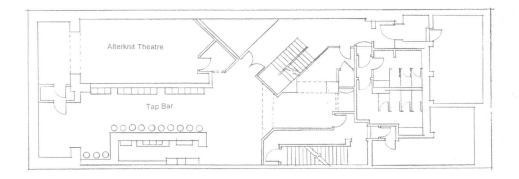

first-floor performance space with its bal-cony, and the 80-seat Alterknit Theatre. The bars cater to a variety of tastes. Microbrewed beers are offered at The Tap Bar; coffee, espresso, and tea are the order of the day at The Front Bar.

A staircase opens to all levels. Budgetary considerations encouraged the use of many items which were on the premises before renovation. While some props were moved from the original club site, other sewing machines and spinning wheels were yard sale and antique shop "finds."

The ANA Hotel

Ocean Club

"If nothing else, the past two decades have seen a dramatic decline in alcohol consumption. Therefore, it is critical that nightspots offer something to their guests other than just liquor. Depending on location, hotel affiliation, and customer profile, there needs to be an emphasis on ambiance, entertainment, sports, comfort, friendliness and food."

—*Interior Design Force*

Courtyard Bar

International Crossroads Sheraton

Azur

Wave Bar

"…Bars are having to offer alternative activities and entertainment, from acoustic music to poetry readings to virtual reality computer games. The bar/poolroom concept has increased in popularity as well. The biggest change to the late night scene is the advent of coffee houses, which are replacing bars as the hip hang-out spot. Another trend seems to be the multiplex facility."

—*KRA, Inc.*

The Westin Hotel Lounges

SALUD!

LOUNGES WORLDWIDE

The ANA
SAN FRANCISCO, CALIFORNIA
San Francisco

Moderne with a masculine feeling, ANA Hotel's lobby lounge presents a pleasingly precise look. Design details include a brushed gold-leaf rotunda, a Lalique-inspired chandelier, and contemporary artwork by David Hockney, Roy Lichtenstein, and Robert Motherwell. Geometric patterns abound—circles, squares, diamonds, and stripes. The sculptural aspects of accessory pieces, lamps, and small tables add to the 1930s feeling. There are genteel references to games, too. Playing cards are pictured on upholstery fabrics and in displayed artwork; subtle checkerboard-style bar stool backs, and even a credenza with insets reminiscent of a backgammon board contribute to the feeling. Formerly a Le Meridien property, this hotel in San Francisco's Yerba Buena district remained fully operational during a fast-track renovation process which included reconfiguring the first floor to create a feeling of spaciousness.

Owner: **ANA Enterprises, Ltd.** Designers: **Bob Barry, Cynthia Forchielli, Helen Glynn, Jackie Barry, Bernie Miranda of Barry Design Associates, Inc.** Architects: **William A. Karst, Craig Davenport, Robin L. Holt-Henry of The Callison Partnership** Square Footage: **4,200** (lobby/reception area) **50,000** (public areas) Opened: **1992** Photographer: **John Sutton**

The Westin Hotel
PROVIDENCE, RHODE ISLAND
Lounges

Talk about offering something for everybody, The Westin Hotel in Providence, Rhode Island, provides a Sports Lounge, a Library Lounge, and a Jazz Lounge.

The Jazz Lounge, like jazz itself, is softly seductive in its color palette, with lighting that plays a soothing part. Positioning of the bar stools and freestanding tables and chairs maximizes the limited space in a way that contributes to the intimacy of the setting. A view of the Providence skyline gives hotel guests a sense of locale as they experience live performances by area jazz artists.

By contrast, the sports theme draws locals and hotel guests who want to cheer the team of their choice in the Sports Lounge environment. Sports memorabilia from local and university teams, as well as TV monitors for viewing games, establish the mood.

Finally, for those in a contemplative mood, the leather-upholstered furniture and padded fabric walls of the Library Lounge make for an inviting respite. Conversation and cocktails are well-suited to the sumptuous surroundings, replete with details such as parquet flooring and wood marquetry.

Owner: **Rhode Island Convention Center Authority** Designer: **Robert DiLeonardo of DiLeonardo International, Inc.** Architect: **The Nichols Partnership** Square Footage: **376,684** (hotel) Design Budget: **Approximately $54 million** (hotel) Opened: **1994** Photographer: **Warren Jagger**

International Crossroads
MAHWAH, NEW JERSEY
Sheraton

Everywhere the eye wanders, there's something satisfying to see. Design creates the sense of perpetual activity at this discotheque nightclub in International Crossroads Sheraton hotel. The idea was to provide a space within the hotel that would draw a singles crowd from the local community. Reflective portions of the ceiling pick up the black and white checkerboard flooring and accent tiles. Chairs and bar stools accentuate the white trim used elsewhere throughout the space—in railings around the room and above the bar, and in the distinctive decorative planters, for instance. A marigold and turquoise color scheme adds yet another lively note.

Owners: **Prime Motor Inns** Designers: **Stephen D. Thompson, ASID; Bob Goldberg, ASID of Interior Design Force** Architects: **John Gilchrist, Robert Gilchrist, M. Callori of The Gilchrist Partnership** Square Footage: **1,900** Design Budget: **$130,000** Seats: **121** *(nightclub)* Opened: **1988** Photographer: **Peter Paige**

Luminous and refined, Azur is like a beacon that beckons guests to stop and catch their breath. Beautiful blues of sea and sky mirror the allure of the Côte d'Azur at this 17,000-square-foot facility. Azur occupies an atrium space within the Galviidae Common shopping complex in Minneapolis, and the atrium influence has shaped its sophisticated, softly glowing interior.

Azur consists of a lounge, bar, fine dining area, deli cafeteria, and a ballroom/conference center, all built around a five-story atrium. The glitter of glass and reflective surfaces, such as stainless steel and mirrors, are balanced by the pleasant glow of backlighting. Etched glass-topped tables lining the curved freestanding glass wall are internally illluminated. Bottles and glassware decorate the mirrored back wall of the bar, the

the bar, the center of which is etched with a blue logo. Meanwhile, the bar itself is made of perforated metal and acrylic, with purple backlighting. The bar and adjoining leather-furnished lounge are separated by a dropped soffit and curved cove.

Owner: **D'Amico & Partners** Architects: **Gregory Rothweiler, Shea Architects, Inc.** Designers: **Richard D'Amico, D'Amico & Partners** Square Footage: **17,000** Design Budget: **$1,700,000** Seats: **512** Opened: **1990** Photographer: **Christian Korab**

Ocean
Club

It's the 1930s and guests are gathered in a cruise ship's great room: that's the design premise at the curvaceous Ocean Club, where an art deco influence sweeps across the interior like a Caribbean breeze. Railings surround raised seating areas, and portholes provide a peek into fish tanks. Because the room is only used at night, murals and aquariums were introduced to create a view. Curving forms are found in the granite bar, and again in the blue neon-trimmed soffits. A dance floor and stage area are part of the nightclub's attractions at Sugar Bay Plantation Resort.

Designers: **Stephen D. Thompson, ASID;
Bob Goldberg, ASID of Interior Design
Force** Architect: **Archeon, Inc.** Square
Footage: **50,000** *(entire project)* Design
Budget: **$22/sq. ft.** Seats: **112** (nightclub)
Opened: **1992** Photographer: **Peter Paige**

Wave Bar

Owner: **Jerry's Caterers** Designer: **Deborah Derby, KRA, Inc.** Architect: **Steven L. Kippels, KRA, Inc.** Consultant: **J. Pendergast, Taxis** Square Footage: **2,500** Design Budget: **$150/sq. ft.** Seats: **84** Opened: **1993** Photographer: **© Rion Rizzo/Creative Sources Photography/Atlanta**

Full of flowing curves suggesting waves, and awash with shades of blue, the interior of the main airport lounge at Daytona Beach Regional Airport looks as restorative as a plunge into a cool swimming pool. Overhead, lighting fixtures create the illusion of suspended bubbles. The design team chose fantasy and water themes to create a lounge area able to withstand the rigors of high traffic. As a result, durability joins forces with drama at Wave Bar. Classic 1950s-style bar stools and chairs are covered with iridescent vinyl, and the polished white stone bar and tabletops are meant to withstand spills.

Blue hues of the bar area flooring flow over into swirls of Axminster carpet. Sinuously curving banquettes seem to restate the wave shapes on the mosaic-tiled bar front. Similarly, curves of the bar area ceiling soffit, inset with reflective vinyl wallcovering, are repeated in the bar top scallop design. Reflective back bar tiles carry through the watery wave theme.

Courtyard Bar

Airports being the high-traffic, high-turnover places they are—and the Daytona Beach Regional Airport is no exception—the welcoming aspects of Courtyard Bar are quite an achievement. Copper, stone, wrought iron furnishings, and wood combine to create a comfortable setting. Inviting lighting at the curving canopied copper bar and the warmth of wood are just a couple of the soothing touches at this spot. Created for client Jerry's Caterers, the interior inspiration was based on demographic research that determined the customer base consists primarily of the elderly and the business traveler.

The look of luxury leaves a lasting impression for customers on the go. In fact, the Courtyard Bar (also called the Canopy Bar) resembles a resort hotel lobby. There's a certain richness in the mottled effect of green and purple slate flooring, and the curving banquette beckons guests to relax and stay awhile. Practicality and durability were motivators in selecting finishes, fabrics, and wallcoverings for the interior. Vinyl wall-covering and seat upholstery, sealed slate flooring, and real wood veneers that were fabricated as high pressure laminates are a few examples.

Owner: **Jerry's Caterers** Designer: **Deborah Derby, KRA, Inc.** Architect: **Steven L. Kippels, KRA, Inc.** Consultant: **J. Pendergast, Taxis** Square Footage: **1,000** Design Budget: **$150/sq. ft.** Seats: **22** Opened: **1993** Photographer: © **Rion Rizzo/ Creative Sources Photography/Atlanta**

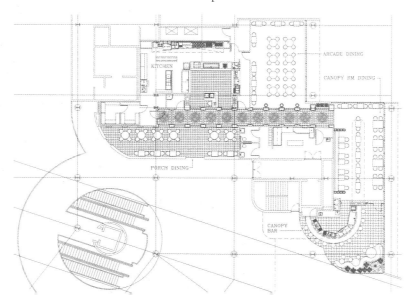

Bitter End

Bistro & Brewry

Franklin Street Brewing Company

Brew Moon

"The current trends are to be theatrical and highly theme-driven....It is not enough to create atmosphere, one has to create new experience in order to compete. Over the past two decades, drinking establishments have changed from simply comfortable, pleasant places to relax to a form of entertainment itself...."
—*Darlow Christ Architects, Inc.*

Gramercy Tavern

ON TAP

TAVERNS & BREWPUBS

Bitter End

AUSTIN, TEXAS

Bistro & Brewery

Like a streak of static electricity zapping its way along the length of the bar wall, a 30-foot-long neon sculpture by Austin artist Ben Livingston provides a visual burst of energy at Bitter End. It's not surprising, though, that the brew house with its copper tanks remains the focal point of the space. Green corrugated metal at the entrance and galvanized industrial lighting fixtures are in keeping with the shape and style of brewing tanks. Copper tabletops, as well as booth and bar area copper accents, provide continuity. Salvaged longleaf yellow pine (hard pine) was used for woodwork and trim; the bar top and casework also feature the same type of wood.

The early 1900s structure formerly housed a teen nightclub. For this project, the building was stripped down to foot-thick, load-bearing exterior walls; overhead, wooden trusses were revealed when layers of paint were sandblasted away. Dick Clark Architecture preserved the building's original character, applying only clear sealer to walls and trusses, and staining the concrete floor. Bitter End draws a variety of clientele from, among other places, the state capitol and the nearby University of Texas.

Owner: **Reed Clemons** Architects: **Dick Clark, Heidi Goebel, Chris Lewis, Peter Green of Dick Clark Architecture** Consultants: **Jerry Garcia, P.E.; Jerry Fleming** Contractor: **Beth Wynn, Pinnacle Construction** Square Footage: **5,600** Design Budget: **$625,000** Seats: **200** Opened: **1994** Photographer: **Paul Bardagjy**

Brew Moon

Brew Moon stands at that fork in the road where nature meets technology and science makes friends with romance. It offers customers craft-brewed beer made on the premises, but unlike many brewpubs, the design focuses on the taste rather than the technology of beer-making.

Brew Moon's palette blends romantic shades of blue and purple with "beer color" accents of gold, amber, and copper. Textured woods and curved glass panels add character. Abstract lunar references are achieved through the use of light and texture, evident in floor, wall, and ceiling elements. Three walls make reference to the textures, materials, and flowing forms that represent characteristics of beer. Back-lit bands of cast glass pierce the cylindrical forms that hint at beer's translucence, and a custom frieze illustrates the making of craft-brewed beer. Brew Moon sits in the heart of Boston's theater district.

Design Team: **Peter G. Darlow,**
Catherine A. Christ of Darlow Christ
Architects, Inc. Graphic Design: **Anita**
Meyer, plus design inc. Construction:
Cafco Seats: **240-260** Opened: **1994**
Photographer: **Anton Grassl**

Gramercy Tavern

Two hundred years ago and turn-of-the-next millennium—that's the hybrid sense of time and neighborhood evident at Gramercy Tavern. A little history and a little mystery amplify the design, which draws from the rustic aspects of early American architecture, as well as the existing Beaux-Arts details and grid layout of the department store that formerly occupied the space. The design team took advantage of the 20-foot by 20-foot bays to establish three dining areas, each with its own character, in addition to a cozy private dining room. The client desired an intimate space that recalled Early American taverns, something the designers achieved by relying on interpretation rather than imitation.

Throughout the interior, a horizontal zone of unifying elements ties the space together, although ceilings and materials are different in each room. Contributing to the tavern character of the bar area are the subtly curving bar constructed of brushed copper and black-stained oak, beamed ceilings, a vibrant mural, and a brick rotisserie. There's a distinct library-of-liquor-bottles look to the black-stained wine cabinets that outline the entranceway to one of the dining rooms. The 10,000 square feet of space is divided between the first floor restaurant and the basement where a prep kitchen, wine room, staff offices, and mechanical equipment are housed.

Owners: **Danny Meyer, Larry Goldenberg, Tom Colicchio** Designers/Architects: **Peter Bentel, Paul Bentel, Susan Nagle, Carol Rusche of Bentel & Bentel, Architects/ Planners A.I.A.** Square Footage: **10,000** (*2 floors*) Design Budget: **$2,000,000** Seats: **60** (*tavern*), **136** (*restaurant*) Opened: **1994** Photographer: **Eduard Hueber/Arch Photo**

Franklin Street Brewing Company

Enduring yet energetic describes the look of Franklin Street Brewing Company. Industrial materials, appropriate for a 100-year-old foundry building, add style that's also in keeping with the brewpub theme. This nightclub/ dining spot features pool playing, dancing, a disc jockey on weekends, and outdoor dining areas available during warm weather months. The age of the building lends a sense of timelessness, and local touches impart a friendly neighborhood feeling. Local artist James Labadie created the murals. Brick walls, a bright yellow back bar, and a 30-foot-long metal-topped bar blend together in a solid statement. Tabletops of galvanized steel and copper are on iron bases salvaged from a local ice cream shop.

At the time it opened, state laws did not allow joint ownership of a retail outlet and a brewery, so a Michigan brewery produces four varieties of beer exclusively for Franklin Street Brewing Company. These include BC Pilsner, BC Light, North of the Border Porter, and Transylvania Ale. Within a week of opening, patrons had nicknamed the place BC's.

Owner: **Mark Vincent** Architect: **Ron Rea,
PeterHansRea** Square Footage: **6,600**
Design Budget: **$600,000** Seats: **290**
Opened: **1991** Photographers: **Nancy
Kenney** *(interior)*, **R. Troy Forrest** *(exterior)*

Arcadia Coffee Co.

"Strong design concepts will attract an audience and create a great eating or drinking atmosphere. The ideas must grow out of the type of food or the clientele. People continue to expect value, and the choices of entertainment are broader than ever. This equates to making memorable and festive places to be."

—Haverson Architecture and Design, P.C.

Nobu

Cafe Vienna

Hyatt La Manga Club

Cafe Miami

Rainforest Cafe

Magic Mushroom Bar

Chopstix & Rice

Italian Coffee Co.

Tapas **Barcelona**

"A strong current trend is toward places that capture something bigger than life: a myth, fantasy, or legend. They transport the guest to another time, or place, or frame of mind—the American West, Hollywood, Rock and Roll."

—Marve Cooper Design Ltd.

LAST CALL

SPECIALTY BARS & COFFEE CAFES

Rainforest Cafe/
MALL OF AMERICA, BLOOMINGTON, MINNESOTA
Magic Mushroom Bar

Right away you know this place is unusual, even before you see the whimsical animal barstools. Most of the world's tropical rainforests—lush with fauna and flora—lie near the equator. This one, however, happens to be inside the Mall of America and incorporates a restaurant, bar, and retail area.

Rainforest Cafe captures the sensory essence of tropical rainforests, establishing an environmentally conscious family experience that both entertains and educates. Tabletops are made of a biocomposite material constructed from recycled materials and a soybean resin. Animated snakes, crocodiles, butterflies, and even a tree, help bring the place to life, as do the 28 live tropical birds, and fish swimming in an arched 3,500-gallon walk-through aquarium at the restaurant's entrance. A mist and fog system is in place, and every 25 minutes a simulated tropical rainstorm moves across the restaurant. ("Rainwater" falls into troughs in the custom-made rock formations.) There are also two waterfalls. The Cafe's ventilation system circulates a realistic rainforest floral scent.

The Magic Mushroom Bar, 32 feet in diameter, provides fresh-squeezed juices and coffee for the 5,000-square-foot retail area, and alcoholic beverage service for the 5,000-square-foot restaurant. The bar's liveliness and color are contained beneath the umbrella of a giant mushrom, and a smaller mushroom stands nearby.

Owner: **Steven Schussler, Senior V.P.**
Architect of Record: **Cuningham Hamilton Quiter, P.A.** Design Architect: **Shea Architects, Inc.** Square Footage: **13,800** (total) Seats: **203** (total), **52** (bar) Opened: **1994** Photographers: **©Dana Wheelock** Photo, Bob Perzel

Chopstix
& Rice

Chopstix and Rice eloquently conveys some less obvious elements of Chinese culture in a cliché-killing rather than a rule-breaking way. Its style is as subtle as shades of pigment and parchment. The entrance is placed in accordance with the principles of feng shui, which is the Chinese technique of arranging a structure's elements in a way said to promote harmony, health, and prosperity. A terrazzo floor is inlaid with bronze shapes resembling grains of rice, a form repeated in the rice bowl-inspired ceiling lighting fixture.

A major portion of Chopstix and Rice's business is derived from office workers during the lunch hour. A light, open look is enhanced by the sandblasted pine panels, brushed with bronze paint, that cover dining area walls. Spatial harmony is evident in the variety of table configurations and the eating counter, all of which encourage traffic flow while accommodating groups, or solo diners.

Owner: **Jack Pong** Design Firm: **Yabu Pushelberg** Seats: **110** Design Budget: **$166,000** Opened: **1992** Photographer: **Robert Burley, Design Archive**

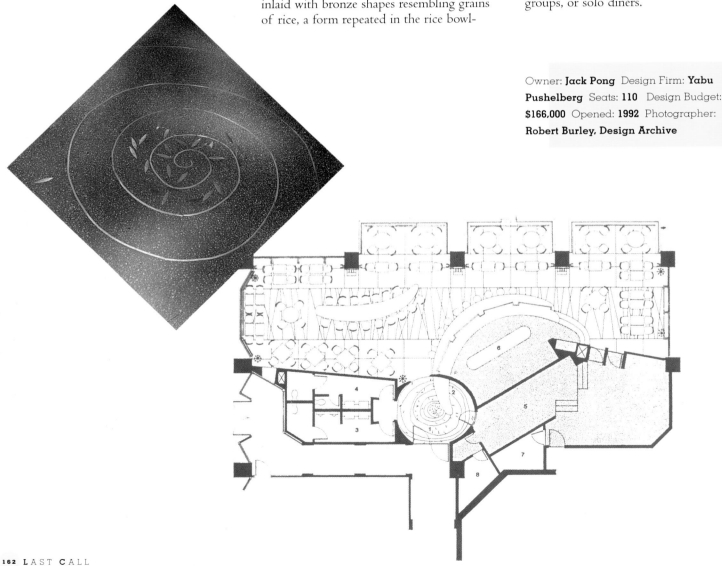

Nobu

Blossoms, branches and stones are expressions of beautiful simplicity at Nobu. Abstract floor-to-ceiling tree sculptures, with the flavor of a Kabuki theater set, first catch the eye. They're fashioned from birch tree trunks, rusted steel plates, and scorched ashwood "branches." Lights in the trees project dramatic shadows. Cherry blossoms stenciled onto the beechwood floors create the effect of having fallen from trees.

The drama of understated natural beauty enlivens this latest, multicultural restaurant concept of Nobu Matsuhisa, Drew Nieporent and Robert DeNiro.

Located in a former bank building in TriBeCa, the interior draws on Nobu Matsuhisa's roots in rural Japan. Custom sconces resembling samurai swords frame the central sushi bar. The backlit green onyx bar features a scorched wood top with bronze and brass details. Upright bar stool supports are shaped like chopsticks. Walls in the room are finished in ceramic tile, rusted steel, and up-lit Japanese riverbed stones. In the private dining room, copper and gold-leaf polka dots play against an indigo backdrop. Sound-absorbing panels, upholstered in golden Italian chenille, hang from birch twigs.

Owners: **Nobu Matsuhisa, Drew Nieporent, Robert DeNiro** Architects: **David Rockwell, Chris Smith, Andrew Fuston of Rockwell Architecture, Planning and Design, P.C.** Square Footage: **2,800** Seats: **74** Opened: **1994** Photographer: **Paul Warchol**

Tapas Barcelona

Starting with six-foot-tall red and yellow letters that spell out its name against a black facade, this concept celebrates the "bar" in Barcelona. Since tapas are Spanish appetizers or snacks, it's fitting that upon entering the space, wall cutouts permit patrons a view of the bright, 12-foot-long tapas bar at the back of the first floor. The festive area is backed by a mirrored mural and enlivened by foodstuff hanging overhead. There's also a 30-foot-long cocktail bar on the main floor.

The city of Barcelona in the Catalan region of Spain was home to Miro, Tapies, Gaudi, and Picasso, so it's not surprising that artwork plays an important role in this interior. Contemporary art, including original gallery and political posters, was brought from Barcelona and suits the Spanish style of Tapas Barcelona. Free-form seating draws from Gaudi's Barcelona park benches.

Tapas Barcelona, which occupies a two-story site that formerly housed another bar/restaurant, was done on a 50-day turn-around. To compensate for the long, narrow space, the design employs curved surfaces and wall cutouts to create a sense of spaciousness. Many elements work together to impart an impression of activity and liveliness. Among them are neon, mirrored disks on the ceiling of the first floor, and a rain forest diorama in the dining room.

Owner: **Restaurant Development Group** Designers: **Marve H. Cooper, Keith W. Curtis, Grace K. Rappe of Marve Cooper Design** Square Footage: **3,300** Design Budget: **$120,000** Seats: **25** *(cocktail bar)*, **8** *(tapas bar)*, **32** *(booth seating)*, **50** *(second-floor dining area)* Opened: **1995** Photographer: **Mark Ballogg, Steinkamp/Ballogg, Chicago**

Hyatt
La Manga Club

Stylish, Spanish, and just right for attracting the diverse clientele of a luxury golf/leisure resort, the Jazz/Tapas Bar at Hyatt La Manga Club has twice the ordinary appeal. That's because the facility features two bars, both with built-in ambiance. Just as the tapas dining concept allows guests to sample those small, tasty plates of tidbits, the tapas bar derives its character from samplings of artwork and appetizing food displays. An island bar in the center of the room provides the focal meeting area that one might expect to find in a Spanish saloon.

Entertainment at the island bar includes a piano on a raised stage, and a video screen. Chairs are a mix of rustic and contemporary, wood and metal. Rich red ceilings, vivid yellow walls, and upholstery fabrics on bar stools that pick up colors of locally produced tiles help tie the look together. Curved metal railings add a sophisticated note.

Client: **Boris Abroad Ltd.** Design Team: **Harry Gregory, Zoran Dzunic, Pippa Ayres, Roy el Khoury of Gregory Aeberhard PLC** Architect: **Wimberly, Allison, Tong & Goo** Square Footage: **2,616** Design Budget: **£80,000** Seats: **84 + 30 + 30** Opened: **1993** Photographer: **Robert Miller**

Cafe Miami
at Bloomingdale's

KENDALL, FLORIDA

Owner: **Federated Department Stores**
Designer/Architect: **Bryan Gailey, FRCH Design Worldwide (formerly SDI/HTI)**
Square Footage: **600** Seats: **28** Opened: **1993** Photographer: **Peter Paige**

Coffee shop amenities are part of today's retail details, and Cafe Miami is a stylish and upbeat example of the current trend. As one might guess from its name, the cafe is located a short distance from Miami. The pastel impression created by the interior is as soothing as soft, harmonious music. A pink glow emanates from the bar area, drawing the eye across a bright white seating space. Chair upholstery provides another touch of color. Higher tables give the impression of offering a good people-watching perch, while lower ones are well-suited to relaxation and conversation.

Cafe Vienna
CHICAGO, ILLINOIS
at Marshall Field's

Cafe Vienna within Marshall Field's department store borrows its name from Vienna, and bows to the straightforward *Wiener Werkstaette Vienna* design influence. In addition, this design recalls the grid patterns prevalent during the era of Josef Hoffmann, whose influence is also evident in the stylish simplicity of bar stools, tables, and chairs. Tile designs as well as sleek pendant lamps hanging over the bar contribute to the uncluttered interior. Adjacent to the store's food court, this 25-seat cafe provides a coffee-drinker's getaway. It's the ideal environment for shoppers who wish to re-energize while indulging in the American passion for coffee and coffee-based specialty drinks.

Owner: **Dayton Hudson** Designer/ Architect: **Martin Anderson, FRCH Design Worldwide (formerly SDI/HTI)** Square Footage: **400** Seats: **25** Opened: **1988** Photographer: **Don DuBroff**

Arcadia
DARIEN, CONNECTICUT
Coffee Co.
OLD GREENWICH, CONNECTICUT

Today's coffee culture encompasses all sorts of cafes, from frenetic grab-and-go places, to those where customers can sit around sipping cappuccino and discussing cyberspace. Both Arcadia Coffee Company locations boast an open and inviting environment in which one can sit and converse comfortably.

The Arcadia in Darien is splashed with shades of cranberry, mustard yellow, and leaf green. Located on a corner, adjacent to a theater, this small room formerly housed props. The application of appetizing food colors and the use of shapes, such as the boomerang coffee bar with its zinc countertop, create a sense of significance in this 800-square-foot space.

Stencil work on the floor and walls of the Old Greenwich location enabled the designers to create bold and playful patterns within the limited budget. Brightly colored chairs make for an upbeat setting.

Owner: **Caitlin McVarish-Tunioli**
Designers: **Jay M. Haverson, Robert Cardello, Ingunn Haralds of Haverson Architecture and Design, P.C.** Architect: **Jay M. Haverson, Haverson Architecture and Design, P.C.** Stencilling: **Julie Lipton-Schwerner** Square Footage: **800** Seats: **30** Opened: **1995** Design Budget: **$75,000** Photographer: **Paul Warchol Photography**

Owner: **Caitlin McVarish-Tunioli**
Designers: **Jay M. Haverson, Andrew Fusto**
of **Haverson Architecture and Design, P.C.**
Architect: **Jay M. Haverson, Haverson**
Architecture and Design, P.C. Stencilling:
Julie Lipton-Schwerner Square Footage:
1,**800** Seats: **30** Opened: **1993** Design
Budget: **$85,000** Photographer: **Paul**
Warchol Photography

Italian Coffee Co.

GLENDALE, ARIZONA

Making the most of the mall milieu, this inviting setting draws the eye in much the same way as a sidewalk cafe. It offers a respite from the bustle of a retail environment, yet relies on the energy of people-watching. Double French doors are thrown open in welcome, and the partially open transom windows above contribute to the sense of inviting the outdoors inside.

Intimacy is lent to the space by combining a variety of light sources. Recessed downlighting provides illumination, pendant-mounted halogen fixtures spotlight the food, and wall-washers highlight displays and special touches such as the mottled paint finishes. A stylish slate tile floor, metal cafe furniture, and ceiling fans that provide a breeze of air circulation all work together to complete the sidewalk cafe ambiance.

Owners: **Max and Mete Sahin** Architects: **Jeffrey Rausch, Kim Dudley of Miller Rausch Interior Architecture** Square Footage: **1,277** Design Budget: **$125,000** Seats: **46** Opened: **1993** Photographer: **Michael Norton**

APPENDIX

PROJECTS

The ANA San Francisco
ANA Hotel
50 Third Street
San Francisco, California 94103
(415) 974-6400

Arcadia Coffee Co.
1069 Boston Post Road
Darien, Connecticut 06820
(203) 655-1606

Arcadia Coffee Co.
Arcadia Road
Old Greenwich, Connecticut 06870
(203) 637-8766

Art Bar & Cafe
14902 Preston Road, #700
Dallas, Texas 75210
(214) 458-0458

Azur
600 Nicollet Mall
Minneapolis, Minnesota 55402
(612) 342-2500

The Big Life
Fukuoka Dome
Fukuoka, Japan

Bitter End Bistro & Brewery
311 Colorado Street
Austin, Texas 78701
(512) 478-2337

Bolo
23 East 22nd Street
New York, New York 10010
(212) 228-2200

Bossa Nova
1960 North Clybourn
Chicago, Illinois 60610
(312) 248-4800

Brew Moon
115 Stuart Street
City Place/Transportation Building
Boston, Massachusetts 02116
(617) 742-5225

Cafe Miami at Bloomingdale's
The Falls Shopping Center
Kendall, Florida 33176
(305) 252-6300

Cafe Vienna at Marshall Field's
111 North State Street
Chicago, Illinois 60602
(312) 781-1000

Carolines Comedy Club
1626 Broadway
New York, New York 10036
(212) 956-0101

Chopstix and Rice
#1 Adelaide Street East
Toronto, Ontario, Canada M5C 2V9
(416) 363-7423

Club Clearview
2806 Elm Street
Dallas, Texas 75220
(214) 939-0006

Cornerstone Grill
600 Brea Mall Drive
Brea, California 92626
(714) 990-2094

Country Star
1000 Universal Center Drive
Universal City, California 91608
(818) 762-3939

Courtyard Bar
Jerry's Caterers
Daytona Beach International Airport
Daytona Beach, Florida 32124
(904) 255-0600

Diamond Jim's Premium Place
Trop/World Casino &
Entertainment Resort
Atlantic City, New Jersey 08401
(609) 340-4029

Empire Ballroom
641 West 17th Street
Costa Mesa, California 92626
(714) 631-8349

Franklin Street Brewing Co.
1560 Franklin
Detroit, Michigan 48207
(313) 568-0390

Gotham Hall
1431 Third Street Promenade
Santa Monica, California 90401
(310) 394-8865

Gramercy Tavern
42 East 20th Street
New York, New York 10003
(212) 477-0777

Hyatt La Manga Club
30385 Los Belones
Cartagena, Murcia, Spain
968-564511

International Crossroads Sheraton
Sheraton Hotel
1 International Boulevard
Mahwah, New Jersey 07495
(201) 529-1660

Iridium
44 West 63rd Street
New York, New York 10023
(212) 582-2121

Italian Coffee Co.
7700 West Arrowhead Towne Center,
Suite 1034
Glendale, Arizona 85308
(602) 979-0083

Ivory
69 Yorkville Avenue
Toronto, Ontario, Canada M5R 1B8
(416) 977-9929

Joe Rockhead's Rockbottom
212 King Street West
Toronto, Ontario, Canada M5H 1K5
(416) 977-8448

JUdson Grill
152 West 52nd Street
New York, New York 10019
(212) 582-5252

Knitting Factory
74 Leonard Street
New York, New York 10013
(212) 219-3006

La Placita
1301 Times Square Causeway Bay
Hong Kong
(852) 506-3308

Luna Notte
6402 North New Braunfels
San Antonio, Texas 78209
(210) 822-4242

Magic Mushroom Bar/Rainforest Cafe
Bloomingdale Atrium, First Floor
Mall of America
Bloomington, Minnesota 55425
(612) 339-7006

Manhattan Express
Hotel Rossiya
Moscow, Russia
7-095-298-5355

Monkey Bar
60 East 54th Street
New York, New York 10022
(212) 838-2600

Nobu
105 Hudson Street
New York, New York 10013
(212) 219-0500

Nola's Cocina Mexicana
Biltmore Fashion Park
2590 East Camelback Road
Phoenix, Arizona 85016
(602) 957-8393

Ocean Club
Sugar Bay Plantation Resort
Smith Bay Road
St. Thomas, USVI 00802
(809) 777-7100

Orchid, The Nightclub
117 Peter Street
Toronto, Ontario, Canada M5V 2G9
(416) 598-4990

Planet Hollywood, Reno
200 North Virginia Street
Reno, Nevada 89501
(702) 323-7837

Rainbow!
30 Rockefeller Plaza,
64th and 65th Floors
New York, New York 10112
(212) 632-5000

Rio Rio Cantina
409 East Commerce Street
San Antonio, Texas 78205
(210) 226-8462

Ruby Tuesday
1763 Beach Boulevard
Biloxi, Mississippi 39531
(601) 432-2223

Spago, Las Vegas
The Forum Shops at Caesars
Las Vegas, Nevada 89109
(702) 369-6300

Spinnakers
207 Queens Quay
West Harbourfront
Toronto, Ontario, Canada M5J 1A7
(416) 203-0559

Starbuck's
Route 132
Hyannis, Massachusetts 02601
(508) 718-6767

Tang's Ginger Cafe
1310 Hennepin Avenue
Minneapolis, Minnesota 55403
(612) 339-9220

Tapas Barcelona
111 West Hubbard
Chicago, Illinois 60610
(312) 467-1091

Wave Bar
Jerry's Caterers
Daytona Beach International Airport
Daytona Beach, Florida 32124
(904) 255-0600

The Westin Hotel Lounges
The Westin Hotel
1 West Exchange Street
Providence, Rhode Island 02903
(401) 598-8000

Winning Streak® Sports Grill
Harrah's Casino Complex
One Riverboat Drive
North Kansas City, Missouri 64116
(816) 472-7777

ARCHITECTS/DESIGNERS

Gregory Aeberhard PLC
Interior Architectural Design
Berkshire House 168/173
High Holborn
London, England WCIV 7AA
Phone: (171) 465-8855
Fax: (171) 465-8856

Archeon, Inc.
3071 Director's Row
Memphis, Tennessee 38131
Phone: (901) 345-3244

Barry Design Associates, Inc.
11601 Wilshire Boulevard, Suite 102
Los Angeles, California 90069
Phone: (310) 478-6081
Fax: (310) 312-9926

Bentel & Bentel Architects/Planners A.I.A.
22 Buckram Road
Locust Valley, New York 11560
Phone: (516) 676-2880
Fax: (516) 676-2141

Bromley Caldari Architects PC
242 West 27th Street
New York, New York 10001
Phone: (212) 620-4250
Fax: (212) 620-4502

The Callison Partnership
1420 Fifth Avenue, #2400
Seattle, Washington 98101
Phone: (206) 623-4646

Dick Clark Architecture
207 West Fourth Street
Austin, Texas 78701
Phone: (512) 472-4980
Fax: (512) 472-4991

Concept Nouveau, Inc.
2803 Main Street
Dallas, Texas 75226
Phone: (214) 939-0224
Fax: (214) 939-0006

Cool Mission III
14902 Preston Road, #700
Dallas, Texas 75240
Phone: (214) 458-0458
Fax: (214) 458-1109

Marve Cooper Design
2120 West Grand Avenue
Chicago, Illinois 60612
Phone: (312) 733-4250
Fax: (312) 733-9715

Cuningham Hamilton Quiter, P.A.
201 Main Street Southeast, Suite 325
Minneapolis, Minnesota 55414

D'Amico & Partners
275 Market Street
Minneapolis, Minnesota 55405

Darlow Christ Architects, Inc.
2326 Massachusetts Avenue
Cambridge, Massachusetts 02140
Phone: (617) 497-9191
Fax: (617) 497-9090

DiLeonardo International, Inc.
2350 Post Road
Warwick, Rhode Island 02886
Phone: (401) 732-2900
Fax: (401) 732-5315

Engstrom Design Group
1414 Fourth Street, Suite 200
San Rafael, California 94901
Phone: (415) 454-2277
Fax: (415) 454-2278

Orli Eshkar Architect
767 Lexington Avenue
New York, New York 10021
Phone: (212) 755-1505
Fax: (212) 755-5163

FRCH Design Worldwide
      (formerly known as SDI/HTI)
311 Elm Street
Cincinnati, Ohio 45202
Phone: (513) 241-3000
Fax: (513) 241-5015

FRCH Design Worldwide
      (formerly known as SDI/HTI)
860 Broadway
New York, New York 10003
Phone: (212) 254-1229
Fax: (212) 982-5543

The Gilchrist Partnership
135 Fort Lee Road
Leonia, New Jersey 07605
Phone: (201) 461-8606

Haigh Architects
125 Greenwich Avenue
Greenwich, Connecticut 06830
Phone: (203) 869-5445
Fax: (203) 869-5033

Hardy Holzman Pfeiffer Associates
902 Broadway, 19th Floor
New York, New York 10010
Phone: (212) 677-6030
Fax: (212) 979-0535

Hatch Design Group
3198 D Airport Loop Drive
Costa Mesa, California 92626
Phone: (714) 979-8385
Fax: (714) 979-6430

Haverson Architecture & Design
289 Greenwich Avenue
Greenwich, Connecticut 06830
Phone: (203) 629-8300
Fax: (203) 629-8399

Haverson/Rockwell Architects, P.C.
(see Haverson Architecture & Design, and
Rockwell Architecture, Planning and
Design)

Martin Hirschberg Design Associates Ltd.
334 Queen Street East
Toronto, Ontario, Canada M5A 1S8
Phone: (416) 868-1210
Fax: (416) 868-6650

Hnedak Bobo Group
104 South Front Street
Memphis, Tennessee 38103
Phone: (901) 525-2557
Fax: (901) 525-2570

Interior Design Force
42 Greene Street
New York, New York 10013
Phone: (212) 431-0999
Fax: (212) 431-9210

Alexander Isley Design
361 Broadway, Suite 111
New York, New York 10013
Phone: (212) 941-7945
Fax: (212) 226-6332

Knauer Incorporated
741 St. Johns Avenue
Highland Park, Illinois 60035
Phone: (708) 432-0089
Fax: (708) 432-0056

KRA, Inc.
50 Hurt Plaza, Suite 405
Atlanta, Georgia 30303
Phone: (404) 589-8522
Fax: (404) 589-8183

Steven Lombardi
3rd Floor, Flat C
To Li Garden
To Li Terrace
Hong Kong
Phone: (852) 818-4946

Marnell Corrao Associates
4495 South Polaris Avenue
Las Vegas, Nevada 89103
Phone: (702) 739-9413
Fax: (702) 739-8521

Miller Rausch Interior Architecture
1702 East Highland, Suite #404
Phoenix, Arizona 85016
Phone: (602) 235-9440
Fax: (602) 235-9502

Morrison Restaurants, Inc.
4721 Morrison Drive
Mobile, Alabama 36625
Phone: (334) 344-3000
Fax: (334) 343-4365

Jordan Mozer & Associates, Ltd.
228 West Illinois Street, Second Floor
Chicago, Illinois 60610
Phone: (312) 661-0060
Fax: (312) 661-0981

Morris Nathanson Design
163 Exchange Street
Pawtucket, Rhode Island 02860
Phone: (401) 723-3800
Fax: (401) 723-3813

The Nichols Partnership
2600 Douglas Road, Suite 900
Coral Gables, Florida 33134
Phone: (305) 443-5206
Fax: (305) 446-2872

Norwood Oliver Design Associates, Inc.
65 Bleeker Street
New York, New York 10012
Phone: (212) 982-7050
Fax: (212) 674-2302
      and
501 American Legion Way
Pt. Pleasant Beach, New Jersey 08742
Phone: (908) 295-1200
Fax: (908) 899-4680

Pentagram Design
212 Fifth Avenue, 17th Floor
New York, New York 10010
Phone: (212) 683-7000
Fax: (212) 532-0181

PeterHansRea
120 Peabody Street
Birmingham, Michigan 48009
Phone: (810) 540-0520
Fax: (810) 540-2350

Rockwell Architecture, Planning and
Design, P.C.
5 Union Square West
New York, New York 10003
Phone: (212) 463-0334
Fax: (212) 463-0335

Schweitzer BIM
5499 West Washington Boulevard
Los Angeles, California 90016
Phone: (213) 936-6163
Fax: (213) 936-5327

Shea Architects
100 North Sixth Street, #300A
Minneapolis, Minnesota 55403
Phone: (612) 339-2257
Fax: (612) 349-2930

Sprinkle Robey Architects
454 Soledad
San Antonio, Texas 78205
Phone: (210) 227-7722
Fax: (210) 226-0200

Adam D. Tihany International, Ltd.
57 East 11th Street
New York, New York 10003
Phone: (212) 505-2360
Fax: (212) 529-3578

Wimberly Allison Tong & Goo
Second Floor, Waldron House
57 Old Church Street
London, England 5W3 5BS
Phone: (171) 376-3260

Yabu Pushelberg
55 Booth Avenue
Toronto, Ontario, Canada M4M 2M3
Phone: (416) 778-9779
Fax: (416) 778-9747

Yarosch Associates
10 Cape Drive
Mashpee, Massachusetts
Phone: (508) 477-4731

P H O T O G R A P H E R S

Mark Ballogg
Steinkamp/Ballogg Photography, Inc.
6 West Hubbard
Chicago, Illinois 60610
Phone: (312) 421-1233
Fax: (312) 421-1241

Paul Bardagjy
4111 B. Marathon Boulevard
Austin, Texas 78756
Phone: (512) 452-9636
Fax: (512) 452-6425

Brian Barnaud
13415 Spring Grove
Dallas, Texas
Phone: (214) 239-4443
Fax: (214) 239-4443

Robert Burley, Design Archive
276 Carlaw Avenue, Suite 219
Toronto, Ontario, Canada
Phone: (416) 466-0211
Fax: (416) 465-2592

Cameron Carothers
Cameron Carothers Photography
1340 Glenwood Road, #8
Glendale, California 91201
Phone: (818) 246-1057

George Cott/Chroma, Inc.
2802 Azeele Street
Tampa, Florida 33609
Phone: (813) 873-1374
Fax: (813) 871-3448

Don DuBroff
101 South Catherine
La Grange, Illinois 60525
Phone: (708) 482-0945
Fax: (708) 482-0965

Gerdi Eller Photography
115 East Ninth Street, 9J
New York, New York 10003
Phone: (212) 473-8342
Fax: (212) 674-8767

R. Troy Forrest
R. Troy Forrest Photographer
1185 Chicago Road
Troy, Michigan 48083

Andrew Garn
85 East 10th Street
New York, New York 10003
Phone: (212) 353-8434
Fax: (212) 794-3624

Anton Grassl Photographie
5 Sycamore Street
Cambridge, Massachusetts 02140
Phone: (617) 876-1321

Eduard Hueber
Arch Photo
104 Sullivan Street
New York, New York 10012
Phone: (212) 941-9294
Fax: (212) 941-9317

Kerun Ip
6th Floor, 5 HOI Ping Road
Causeway Bay, Hong Kong
Phone: (852) 882-1602
Fax: (852) 882-1644

Warren Jagger
Warren Jagger Photography
150 Chestnut Street
Providence, Rhode Island
Phone: (401) 351-7366
Fax: (401) 421-7567

Richard Johnson
Interior Images by Richard Johnson
100 Woodmount Avenue
Toronto, Ontario, Canada M4C 3Y4
Phone: (416) 467-4620
Fax: (416) 467-9894

Elliott Kaufman
255 West 90th Street
New York, New York 10024
Phone: (212) 496-0860
Fax: (212) 496-9104

Nancy Kenney
Nancy Kenney Photography
1755 Livernois
Troy, Michigan 48083
Phone: (810) 362-5008

Christian Korab
Christian Korab Photography
2757 Emerson Avenue South
Minneapolis, Minnesota 55408
Phone: (612) 870-8947
Fax: (612) 870-9034

Norman McGrath
Norman McGrath Photography
164 West 79th Street, 6C
New York, New York 10024
Phone: (212) 799-6422
Fax: (212) 799-1285

Robert Miller
10929 Howland Drive
Reston, Virginia 22091
Phone: (703) 758-9818

Motoi Niki
Nacasa & Partners, Inc.
3-5-5 Minami-Azabu, Minato-Ku
Tokyo 106, Japan
Phone: 03-3444-2922
Fax: 03-3444-2678

Michael Norton
Michael Norton Photography, Inc.
3106 North 16th Street
Phoenix, Arizona 85016
Phone: (602) 274-8834
Fax: (602) 274-8828

Peter Paige
Peter Paige Associates, Inc.
269 Parkside Road
Harrington Park, New Jersey 07640
Phone: (201) 767-3150
Fax: (201) 767-9263

Bob Perzel
17954 Judicial Road
Lakeville, Minnesota 55044
Phone: (612) 435-2784
Fax: (612) 435-2784

Rion Rizzo
Creative Sources Photography/Atlanta
6095 Lake Forrest Drive, Suite 100
Atlanta, Georgia 30328
Phone: (404) 843-2141
Fax: (404) 250-1807

Scott Rothwall
Scott Rothwall Photography
25 Fremont
Newport Beach, California 92663
Phone: (714) 673-3023

John Sutton
John Sutton Photography
8 Main Street
San Quentin, California 94964
Phone: (415) 258-8100
Fax: (415) 258-8167

Paul Warchol
Paul Warchol Photography
135 Mulberry Street
New York, New York 10013
Phone: (212) 431-3461
Fax: (212) 274-1953

Dana Wheelock Photo
800 Washington Avenue North
Minneapolis, Minnesota 55401
Phone: (612) 333-5110
Fax: (612) 338-0806

Reven T.C. Wurman
80 Varick Street 7A
New York, New York 10013
Phone: (212) 925-8162
Fax: (212) 431-5131

Hank Young
923 West 24th
Kansas City, Missouri 64108
Phone: (816) 221-7376
Fax: (816) 842-4068

INDEX

ACKNOWLEDGMENTS

I acknowledge the support and guidance I've received from the many writers in my family—especially my father and my mother—but also my stepfather, my mother-in-law, and my volunteer proofreaders, Stephen Bellamy and John Stark Bellamy II.

I thank Charles Rust for his advice. I am grateful to Mike DeLuca of *Restaurant Hospitality*, who encouraged me when I undertook this project, and to Randy Siegel, Cindy Barber, and Eric Broder of *Cleveland Free Times*, who gave me a break so I could finish it. I remain grateful to Stephen Michaelides of *Restaurant Hospitality*, who accepted my poetry credits as work experience, and hired me in the first place.

I thank the staff of PBC International, whose talent and professionalism made this project a positive experience.

And finally, I am indebted to the participating architects and designers whose work has brought their clients' dreams to life, and to the photographers whose work has translated that splendor to the pages herein.

—Gail Bellamy, 1995

411-2